JavaScript: The Ultimate Beginners Guide

Start Coding Today

Preface

I want to thank you for buying this book, *"JavaScript: The Ultimate Beginners Guide, Start Coding Today"*.

This book will help you understand what JavaScript is, its importance, and how you can use this knowledge to create your own scripts for your websites.

Unlike other programming language, JavaScript is one crucial part of a website's basic elements.

This specific type of language is made use of by, even the big names in the World-Wide Web (WWW), such as Google, Yahoo and Bing. That's how important JavaScript is.

I know that as a beginner, you may have trouble understanding computer language, so I presented the lessons in a simple manner. I have included images too, to allow you to visualize the codes and remember them more.

Also, I want you to have fun while learning this new and interesting language.

Who knows? You might be able to design your own website in the future.

Hence, let's start learning.

Thanks again for downloading this book, I hope you enjoy it!

Table of content

Chapter 1: Introduction to JavaScript

Surely, you have heard the term 'JavaScript', from time to time, as you browsed online. You're interested to learn all about it, that was why you have obtained this book. Thus, we have to know first, what JavaScript is.

What is JavaScript?

JavaScript is a computer language that web developers and computer programmers use together with HTML and CSS to create and develop interactive websites. It's a 'script' inserted or used only for web purposes, and cannot be used alone. If you're planning to open your own website learning about JavaScript is a wonderful plan.

Nevertheless, you can learn too how to use this essential language even if you're not an expert programmer. All you need is the desire and patience to acquire a new language.

Take note that JavaScript is different from Java. Java is a markup language, in the same category as C or C++, and is more complex than JavaScript.

JavaScript statements

JavaScript commands, or language, or program instructions are called statements. These statements must follow the correct JavaScript syntax for them to be executed properly, and for these statements to display the correct output.

JavaScript statements can be composed of keywords, values, operators, expressions and comments.

Here are other uses of JavaScript. You can:

1. improve the users' experience with an easy, dynamic and responsive interface.

2. resolve browser problems.

3. allow users to work offline.

4. let users promptly load content from the website.

5. create pop-ups or alerts to maximize users' browsing experience on your website/blog.

6. allow users to give feedbacks.

7. inform the user of an error in his entry or request.

8. allow users instant feedback in their activity. An example is when the user is filling up a form online. With the use of JavaScript, the user will be able to know whether he is filling up the form properly.

9. allow users to interact with your website.

10. animate an element in your website for better user experience.

11. create a congruent interface with other web technologies such as, Java, HTML and CSS.

12. use JavaScript with any browser.

13. create a dynamic website by manipulating your website's elements.

Note: Ascertain though that the user has the option to forgo the pop-ups, because some users don't want distractions while browsing.

If you have studied other computer languages, such as Python, Java, CSS and HTML, you will soon discover that there are similarities between the programs. All you have to do is to connect these similarities, work with the other languages, and work through their differences.

Chapter 2: Setting up the Google Chrome Console

As a beginner, you have to learn how to setup and use the console properly. Google Chrome provides a console where you can practice your JavaScript (JS) for free.

Here are the steps:

1. **Download and install Google Chrome**

   You can download Google Chrome from its official website (*www.google.com/chrome*). It will act as your browser.

   Not only can you use it as your console but it also provides a faster website browsing.

   After downloading it, you can now install it. It's preferable if you use your desktop or laptop.

   The instructions for downloading and installing are provided by the website itself, so you won't have any trouble with this step.

2. **Click on the options (brown-yellow circle) found at the right upper portion of the Google Chrome page.**

This will display several options.

See next image:

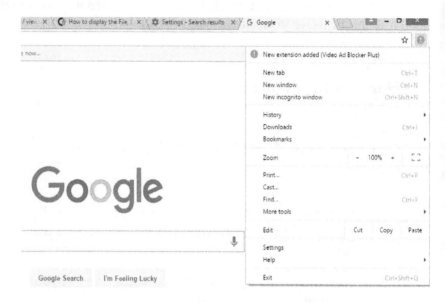

3. **Click on 'More tools',**

4. **Click on 'Developer tools'. Click on 'Console'.**

This will display the console pad with a > symbol. That's where you type your JavaScript. See image below:

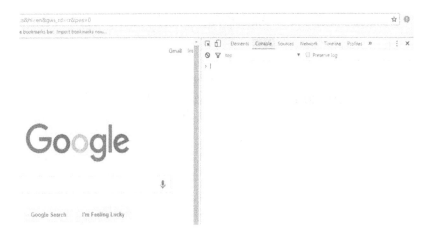

Here's a closer look at the image:

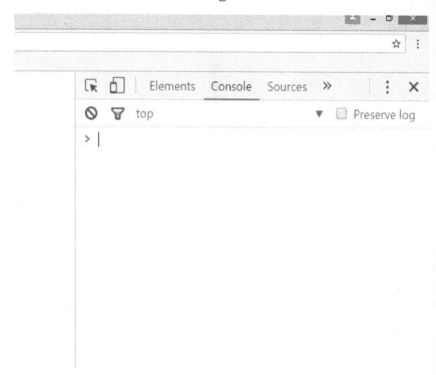

5. **Click on 'Console'.**

This will display the console pad, where you can type your codes. You can enlarge the view if you want. There are also keys/buttons that you can use in deleting or editing your entries.

See image below.

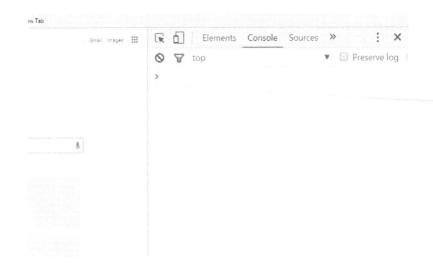

6. You can now start using the console

Explore the JavaScript language in the blank console.

There's a short-cut method in opening your 'Console'.

1. Download and install your Google Chrome in your devise.

2. In the space for your URL address (this is where your http://... is found), type 'about:blank', without the quotation marks.

3. Press 'enter', a totally blank page will appear.

See image below:

Short-cut commands to open the 'Console':

You could also use the short command Ctrl + Shift + J, to open the console.

For Mozilla, you can press F12 on your computer's keypads, and then select 'Console'.

For Mac users, you can use the command Alt J.

4. Next, click on the small square or circle on the upper right hand corner.

This will display the menu, just like in the long method, select 'More tools', then 'Developer tools'.

See next image

5. Select 'More tools', then 'Developer tools'.

Another box will appear. Click on 'Console', to be able to type your JavaScript language.

See next image

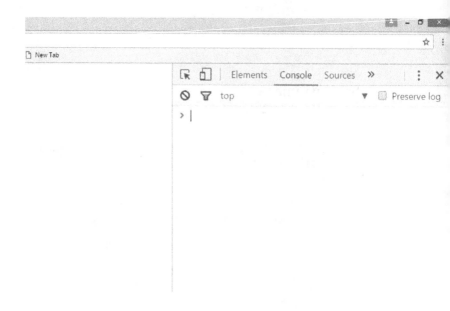

6. You can now login (use console.log ()), and start typing and practicing your JavaScript on the 'Console'. You can explore JavaScript codes and observe how the signs and symbols affect your codes. We'll be having exercises later on in the next chapters, so hold your horses first.

7. You can also click on the 'Preserve log' found at the upper right hand portion of your 'Console' to preserve your messages, while you're working on your codes. But you may prefer not to preserve your logs. It's up to you.

8. You can save your messages by right clicking and then choosing the 'Save as' option on the scroll down.

See next image:

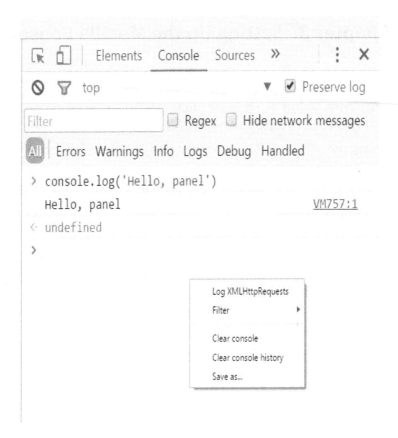

Now, you can start coding!

Chapter 3: Setting Up the Mozilla Console

As mentioned in the previous chapter, you can access your console on Mozilla by clicking F12 on your keypads. This will display your Developer Tools, where you can select 'Console'.

Let's say you have created an alert in your Mozilla 'Console'. See image below:

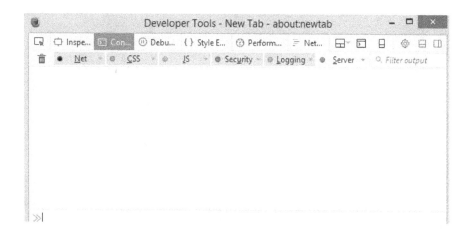

Let's say you want to create an alert.

Example:

alert ("It is my first time to use JavaScript.");

See next image:

No error appeared because the code was correct, thus, the alert will show on your page:

But, if you have a committed an error, such as not using matching quotes, the 'Console' will detect it quickly.

See next image:

The error is indicated, and you have the option to learn more. When you click [Learn More], the link will lead you to a page that explains exactly what was wrong with your code.

In this specific example, the error was because of the unmatched quotes, (the beginning quote is single, while the ending quote is double). You can then proceed to correct your error accordingly.

Chapter 4: Fundamentals of JavaScript

There are fundamental rules of JavaScript that you should remember. You can learn about them as we go on with the chapters, but let's establish first the most important fundamental tenets.

1. **The Unicode character set is used in creating your JavaScript programs.**

   The Unicode character set contains most universal characters, punctuations and symbols. Hence, you can use them easily in writing your statements for your programs to create your JavaScript codes.

2. **You can add the semicolon symbol (;) after each statement.**

   If you're not sure whether to add or not, the best option is to add. You can add the semicolon after each statement.

   In some instances, the browser recognizes the JavaScript code even without the semicolon, but it's still best to add the semicolon to ascertain that the statement is executed properly by any browser. It's not a 'must' but just to be sure.

Example:

alert ("My name is Jekyll.");

3. **You can use a single quote, or double quotes with a string.**

Either the single or the double quotes could be used for strings. But you must ascertain that if you use a single quote before the string, you must also use the single quote after the string. Likewise, with your double quotes. You will know more about strings in chapter 13 to 21.

Example of strings:

'My name is Jekyll. '

"My name is Jekyll. "

4. **There are three primitive types of data.**

These are numbers (1, 21.50, 3.4…), strings ("My name is Jekyll.") and Boolean (true or false).

5. **All numbers are floating-point values.**

Unlike other computer languages, JavaScript doesn't differentiate integers (whole numbers) from floating-point values (numbers with decimal points), because for JavaScript all numbers are floating-point values.

6. **Take note that JavaScript uses the (–) symbol, or hyphen, to subtract and not to connect words.**

Examples: These are not recognized by JavaScript.

student-number

student-name

employee-name

patients-name

7. **You can use the camel case style in naming your variables.**

Camel case can be used by joining two words with the first letter of the first word in lowercase, and the first letter of the second word in uppercase.

Examples:

studentNumber

studentName

employeeName

patientsName

You can also use an underscore to separate names, but it's rarely used.

Examples:

Student_Number

Student_Name

Employee_Name

Patients_Name

8. **You may or may not add white spaces between operators.**

Although, JavaScript doesn't pay attention to white spaces, it's preferable to use white spaces for easy readability.

Examples:

var number = 7;

or var number=7;

Notice that in the first example, there are spaces between the math operator and the number. In the second code, there are no spaces between the math operator (=) and the number.

9. 'Object' is a crucial pillar in JavaScript.

This is due to the fact that objects an include documents, arrays, and a lot of things that you can only find in objects. They have properties and methods. More will be discussed in the other chapters.

10. You can add the JavaScript in the <head> or <body> sections of the HTML page.

However, you have to use the <script> tags; the opening <script> and closing </script> tags.

Your code must be inserted between these opening and closing script tags.

JavaScript can also be placed in external files. This can be accessed, when needed, with a link from your HTML files.

This will result to a faster loading site, and an easier method of reading, identifying, and maintaining the HTML and the JavaScript codes.

Examples will be given in the succeeding chapters.

11. The ideal code length of one line is 80 characters.

This is for easy coding and reading. If you cannot avoid it, and the statement is more than 80 characters, then you have to choose to break the code after an operator.

12. The first character of a JavaScript identifier must be a letter.

It can also be a dollar sign $, and underscore _ but not a number. Identifiers are used to name keywords, variables, labels and functions.

13. There are two types of values.

In JavaScript syntax, there are two types of values: the 'variable' and the 'fixed'. The 'variable' values, as the name implies, have variable (inconstant) values; that's precisely why they are called 'variables.

On the other hand, the 'fixed values have values that remain constant and that don't change. They are called 'literals', as well.

14. Identifiers in JavaScript are case-sensitive.

Be careful in using identifiers because errors can occur when you change the lowercase to uppercase and vice versa.

Examples:

idNumber is different from *idnumber*

The keyword *'var'* is interpreted, but not *'VAR'* or *'Var'*. Always use 'var'. Check the case every time you enter or execute a code.

15. The web browser can execute a JavaScript command in an HTML.

As previously mentioned, JavaScript cannot stand on itself alone; it has to run together with an HTML or CSS. You can either insert the JavaScript into the HTML, or create a link from the HTML to your JavaScript.

Take note that the JavaScript statement is a command or instruction that has to be executed by the web browser.

A JavaScript program can contain various statements waiting to be executed in the order that you wrote them.

16. You can write several statements in one line.

You can do this, but ascertain that each statement is separated by a semicolon.

Examples:

$$x = 2; \quad y = 3; \quad z = x + y;$$

These are the most fundamental rules of the JavaScript computer programming language. As you proceed reading the chapters, you'll discover that there's much more to JavaScript than those mentioned here.

Chapter 5: Important Terms in JavaScript

Every computer language has its own important terms and keywords. JavaScript is no exception. Keywords in JavaScript are considered reserved words.

This is because you cannot use these keywords to name your variables. You have to know these keywords, so you can write your codes correctly.

1. **var** - it declares a variable.

2. **debugger** - it stops the execution of the JavaScript statement, and the debugging function may be accessed.

3. **function** - it indicates a function.

4. **break** – ends a loop or a switch.

5. **for** – it indicates a block of statement that would be executed, when the condition is true.

6. **continue** – it continues a statement at the top, after it has exited from a loop.

7. **if...else** – it indicates a block of statements that would be executed, 'if' the statement is true and -else- if the statement is untrue.

8. **try..catch** – it handles the correction of errors of a block of statements.

31

9. **do/while** – it executes and repeats a block of statements, provided that the condition is true.

10. **switch** – it indicates the execution of a block of statements, based on various cases.

11. **return** – it allows you to exit a function.

12. **loop** – repetition of a function using certain keywords.

Other terms:

1. **foo** – stands for foobar, bar, fubar, or qux. Foobars are metasyntactic variables and act as placeholder for names in computer programming.

   You can use it to retrieve the property value of a variable instead of using the indices. It's useful in accessing values of elements from variables.

   See image below:

```
> Apparel={type: "dress", color: "red"};
< ▶ Object {type: "dress", color: "red"}
> var apparel = {foo: "apparel"};
  var valueFromArrayIndex = apparel[foo];
  var valueFromProperty = apparel.foo;
< undefined
```

2. **push** – this function is another method in adding elements to an array.

Example:

var students = new Array('Damien', 'Lucy', 'Mona', 'Andrew');

students.push('Tom');

If you want to view if your additional element was indeed added, you can use the command:

document.write(students);

This will return this data.

See next image:

Damien,Lucy,Mona,Andrew,Tom

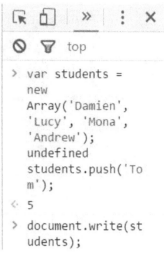

```
> var students =
  new
  Array('Damien',
  'Lucy', 'Mona',
  'Andrew');
  undefined
  students.push('To
  m');
< 5
> document.write(st
  udents);
```

Pointers in using JavaScript keywords

- You can indent your code blocks using 4 spaces.

- Most code blocks are used in functions.

- Remember to use the curly brackets { } with code blocks. Code blocks are group of statements inside the curly brackets.

Chapter 6: Commenting on JavaScript Codes

Albeit, commenting was mentioned in passing in the other chapters. I would like to discuss the commenting styles on JavaScript. This simple action will provide an easier learning experience for beginners, because they can write notes in the JavaScript code anywhere they want to, without ruining the code. This will facilitate the recall of certain data that you may need, as the scripter.

Methods of commenting

Using the double backlash method //

When you want to comment, so you won't forget something on your code, you can simply add the // symbol before your comment.

This sign is typically for single comments.

Example:

var patients = [

"Elsa", //You can create arrays within arrays. (This is a comment.)

"Ana",

"Lily",

"Leo'

]; //This symbol signifies that the statement has ended. (This is a

comment.)

Note: The comments will not be executed by the browser.

Using /* */

This is used when you have multi-lined comments. Just add the /* before the comment and the */ after the comment.

Example:

var patients = {

'Elsa', /*You can create arrays within arrays. Add related elements,

'Ana' such as age, gender, state, and other relevant information to

'Lily' any of these elements.*/

'Leo'
}; //This symbol signifies that the statement has ended. (This is a
comment.)

See image below:

```
File   Edit   Format   View   Help
var patients = {
    'Elsa',    /*You can create arrays within arrays. Add related elements,
    'Ana'        such as age, gender, state, and other relevant information to
    'Lily'       any of these elements.*/
    'Leo"
}

'
```

Reminders:

1. **You can add comments to your statements.**

   You can indicate that the entry is a comment by using the symbols // for one-line comments. When the symbol // appears, the statement will not be executed.

2. **You can also use the same symbol to explain your code.**

   Examples:

   // this is used with a one-liner comment

   Again, for long or multi-line comments with linebreaks, the symbol /* */ is used. When these symbols are used,

37

they prevent the execution of a block of statements, turning them into comments.

The symbols are useful when you're still testing your codes.

Examples:

/* this is a comment with linebreaks */

You need not indicate that it's a comment. The symbols will denote that these are comments that are non-executable.

Even if the line is a code, when you add the // and /* */ symbols they turn into comments, so they won't be executed.

Hence, if you want to omit the execution of a statement, just add these symbols. That's why they are also called comment blocks.

Chapter 7: Debugging Codes

When writing/creating your JavaScript codes, you need to use debugging tools (debuggers) to promptly discover the logical or syntax or errors and resolve them quickly.

What is debugging?

Debugging is a process where a debugger is used to identify and help fix or minimize 'bugs' (errors) in your computer programs.

Your debugger is like a doctor looking for 'illnesses', and then helping the program in 'treating' them.

You don't have to worry because Chrome can provide these tools, since it has a built-in debugger. You can debug your JavaScript by accessing the Chrome dev tools from your menu.

You can quickly access your debugging tool by pressing the F12 key on your keypad, using Mozilla or Chrome.

For the image below. Mozilla is used. The debugger button is found on the upper portion of your tools (Debu…).

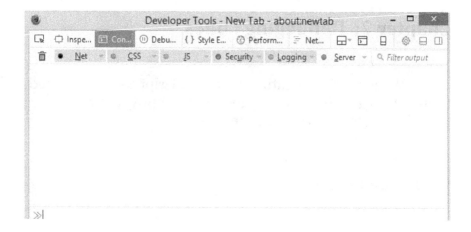

The debugger keyword can stop the execution of the JavaScript.

Example:

*var x = 2*8;*

debugger;

See image below:

```
> var x = 2*8;
< undefined
> debugger;
>
```

This will stop the execution of the JavaScript, and will pause your script until you have debugged and are ready to resume.

You can likewise stop or pause the execution of the JavaScript by setting 'Breakpoints'. You can then evaluate your values, and then proceed whenever you're ready.

If you type the same entries in the Mozilla 'Console', this will appear:

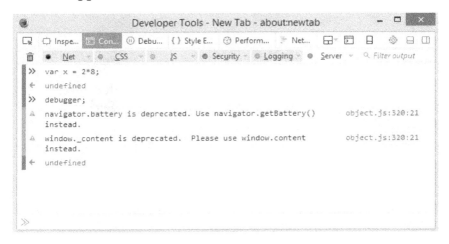

You can click on the 'object.js', and learn how to debug and correct the error.

The window below may also appear, where you can identify the sources, and explore more of the functions of the debugger.

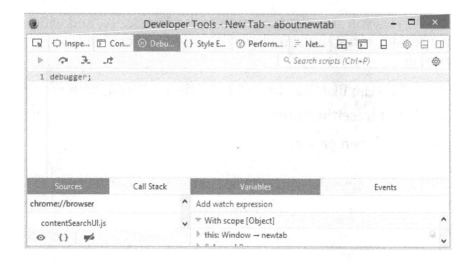

You can now access the specifics of your debugging command, and get information about your JavaScript. Remember that JavaScript is not JAVA.

When you have already created your website, you can use the debugger for more complex corrections of errors.

Chapter 8: JavaScript Functions

Before you can start coding, you will have to learn about how to create your own JavaScript functions. It's because, almost always, your statements will use a function. You cannot write a code without using functions.

In JavaScript, functions have properties and methods, and they are considered as objects because of these characteristics. They must also return a value.

The usual steps in utilizing functions are: calling it and then passing your arguments and waiting for the return value. The arguments can be numbers, strings, or other data types.

Function statement/declarations/definition

This is used to declare a function. You can declare a function by using the function keyword – 'function'. The general formula in declaring a function is:

function functionName (argument1, argument2, argument3...)

{

statement/s to be executed;

}

If you are to insert it in an HTML script, you can write it this way:

```
<script type = "text/javascript">

<!--

function functionName (argument1, argument2,
argument3...)

{

statement/s to be executed;

}

//-->

</script>
```

See image below:

```
File   Edit   Format   View   Help
<script type = "text/javascript">
<!--
function functionName (argument1, argument2, argument3...)
{
statement/s to be executed;
}
//-->
</script>
```

Example 1:

Let's say you want to create a function on calculating the sum of two numbers. You will have first to name your function. For this function, I want to name it gettingSum.

functionName = gettingSum

So, you can create your function (gettingSum) this way:

function gettingSum (x, y)

{

return (x+y);

}

When you need to use it, just type the function name and substitute your numbers, and it will come up with the sum.

See next image:

```
⌖  ⊡  |  Elements   Console   Sources   N

⊘  ▽  top                                ▼

>  function gettingSum (x, y)
   {
        return (x+y);
   }
⤶  undefined

>  gettingSum(19,30);
⤶  49
```

Example 2

This is a function that would greet visitors on your web page.

function greetings()

{

document.write('Welcome to my page!');

}

See image below:

```
> function greetings()
  {
  document.write("Welcome to my page!");
  }
```

This JavaScript code will display your greetings on the your screen.

Example 3

> *function amAlert()*
>
> *{*
>
> *prompt("How are you this morning?");*
>
> *}*

Remember to add the script tags when inserting it into an HTML code:

> *<script type="text/javascript">*
>
> *function amAlert()*
>
> *{*

prompt("How are you this morning? ");

}

</script>

See image below:

```
File  Edit  Format  View  Help
<script type="text/javascript">
function amAlert()
  {
    prompt("How are you this morning?");
    }
</script>
```

How can you insert this functions in your HTML code? This will be discussed in **chapter 36 that explains about how to** insert JavaScript codes into HTML codes.

Example 4

You can use functions in creating a series of alerts. For example, you created an alert that can reflect what's in the mind of your current user. You can create the function through this code:

function knowingYou(x)

{

alert("I dream of "+ x);

}

knowingYou("you");

knowingYou("Paris");

knowingYou("being in love");

See image below:

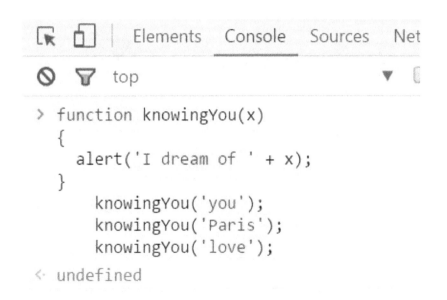

When the code was executed it displayed the 'knowingYou statements specified in the code.

See the series of images below:

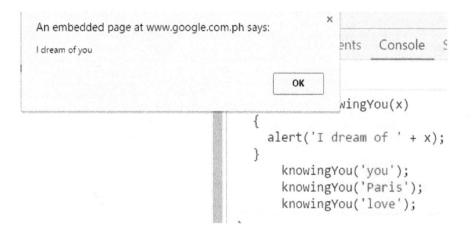

Second statement:

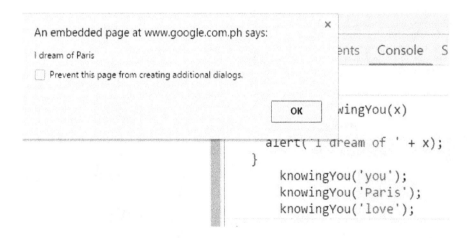

Third statement:

ents   Console

```
wingYou(x)
    alert('I dream of ' + x);
}
        knowingYou('you');
        knowingYou('Paris');
        knowingYou('love');
>
```

You can now call this 'knowingYou' function whenever you want to use it. See? how good JavaScript is in developing interactive little surprises for users on a web page.

Reminders:

- Functions can be utilized several times, provided that you define them first before using them. It would be quick because you only have to define them once.

- Functions are always followed by parentheses and/or brackets.

- Arguments are the same as parameters. Arguments are the names included in the definitions of the function.

- The values will be the return values, after the execution of the statement.

- Functions have Prototype properties.

- You first have to define a function before the browser can 'call' (use) it and execute it.

- You can call a function by creating buttons in the body of your HTML code. This is done by creating a 'form' outside your JavaScript codes to input a button.

Example:

```
<form>

  <input      type="button"      value="press      me"
onclick="amAlert()">

</form>
```

This HTML code will provide a button that has a label "press me" in the web page. When you click on it, the amAlert prompt that we have created earlier will appear.

You can declare as many function as you wish. Just make sure you name them by using variables. You have to remember their names, and know how to use these functions to your advantage.

Chapter 9: Definition and Uses of Variables

As with the other computer languages, JavaScript makes use of variables. Unlike strings, variables are not enclosed in quotes, and you don't have to declare what type they are.

What are variables?

Variables act as 'containers' of your data. Through variables, you can easily store or save your data, and access them later on, when you need them. You can use your data by using the name of the 'container' (variable) to access it. But first, you have to declare and name the variable before you can use or access it.

Uses of variables

They act as containers of your data. They are similar to file names, with their corresponding contents.

The keyword 'var' is used to declare a variable, while the equal (=) sign is used to define the values of the variables.

Example 1:

var x;

x = 1;

Example 2:

var carOwners;

carOwners = "Rachel Newsome", "Luke Tell", "Sarah Colton";

Where:

carOwners is the name of the variable

The names are the values of the variable 'carOwners'.

See image below:

You can now use the variable by using its name only. Let's assume you want to print or display the names on the page; you can use the code: 'document.write'

Example:

document.write(carOwners);

When the command was executed, the names appeared on the page:

See next image:

Rachel
Newsome.Luke
Tell,Sarah
Colton

```
⌞⊀  ⬚     Elements  Console  »              ⋮

⊘  ▽  top                          ▼  ▢ ∣

> var carOwners;
  carOwners = ['Rachel Newsome', 'Luke
  Tell', 'Sarah Colton'];
⟵ ▸ ["Rachel Newsome", "Luke Tell", "Sarah
    Colton"]
> document.write(carOwners);
⟵ undefined
```

Variable initialization

This is the process of storing a value in a variable. You can do it immediately after creating you variable or later on when you want to store it. Indices (0, 1, 1, 3...) will be assigned to each variable, so that you can access them without difficulty. Commonly, variables are initialized with the value – undefined.

Once a variable has been declared, you're not allowed to declare the same variable again.

Creating or declaring variables

You can easily create or declare variables by remembering the following:

- Variables can start with an underscore _ , a dollar sign $, or a letter (lowercase or uppercase), and then after these options, you can use any other symbols or letters.

- The variables must not use keywords. This is understandable. The user will confuse the browser, whether it will execute the user's command or not.

- Use the variable keyword 'var'. Keep in mind to use the lowercase letters.

- It's best to declare your variables before you write your statements or code. If you don't do this, JavaScript will display your variable as 'undefined'. However, the console may execute the command even if the variable is undefined. You will have to discover this from your own browser.

- When assigning values to your variables, use the equal (=) sign. Your values can be a string, a number and other data types.

- It's important to keep in mind that the left-hand side is the variable name and the right-hand side is the value/s of the variable/s. Interchanging them would give you an error.

Example:

var studentName = "Fritzgerald";

The output or return value would be: "Fritzgerald". See image below:

You can also do it this way:

> *var studentName;*
>
> *studentName = 'Fritzgerald';*

See image below:

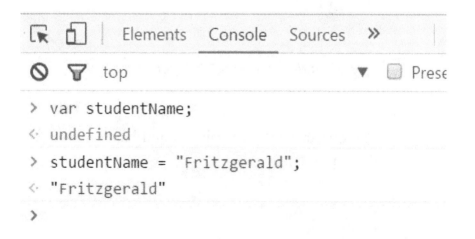

- As previously mentioned, the names of your two-word variables should follow the camel case style (first word is lowercase and the first letter of the second word is in the uppercase.)

Examples:

studentsNames	*previousDate*
studentName	*petName*
patientsName	*homeAddress*
firstName	*schoolID*
lastName	*homeViewers*
idNumber	*lateShow*

If you go over the names above, you will notice that you can name your variables any way you want to.

However, it's better to use a name that you can remember easily because the name describes the content of your variable.

It would be confusing, if you name the data of your car as lastDate, right?

- For the assigned values of your variables, you can use uppercase or lowercase letters, whichever you prefer. But ascertain that the word-strings are enclosed in matching quotes.

Examples:

var patientsName;

patientsName = "Luke Walker";

- You can declare several variables in a single statement by using commas after each variable.

Use the keyword before the name of the variable only. This is usually done in array variables.

Example:

var studentsNames;

studentsNames = ["Fritzgerald", "Walker", "Dixon", "Palmer"];

See next image

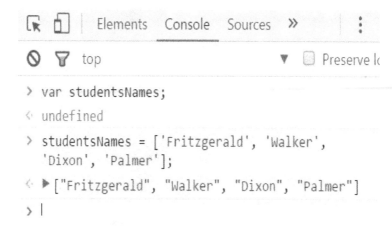

You may want to experiment and see how it appears on the web page. You can use the code:

document.write(studentsNames);

Accessing variables

You can access the values of the variables by its name instead of typing the values of one by one.

See image below:

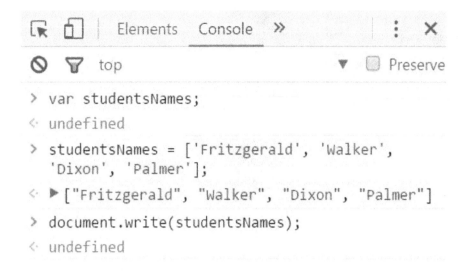

The 'document.write' command will write on the web page the contents of your variable 'studentsNames'. See image below:

Fritzgerald, Walker, Dixon, Palmer

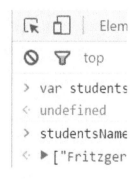

Of course, you can create your code using multiple lines, if you want to. This will depend on your preferences.

Examples of multi-line codes will be discussed more in chapters 29 to 34, on the topic - arrays.

Functions – can allow you to write your code only once and then use it several times.

Basic data types of variables (to be discussed individually in their chapters).

1. Numbers

2. Strings

3. Booleans

4. Objects – Arrays belong here

Reminders:

JavaScript's variables and functions are case-sensitive. Thus, you have to observe the same letter case (uppercase or lowercase) throughout the code.

"studentName" is different from "studentname". You would receive an error when you use a lowercase-name different from the uppercase-name you have entered.

JavaScript is usually 16 digits in length for the web browser to be able to execute the number code properly.

Chapter 10: Basic Data Types of Variables

Variables have four basic data types. These are numbers, strings, Boolean, and objects. We'll skim through these types, because going in-depth in discussing them will leave us not time in learning your JavaScript basic codes.

1. Numbers

In JavaScript, generally, all numbers are considered as 64-bit floating point numbers. When there are no values after the decimal point, the number is presented as a whole number.

Examples:

- *9.000 is presented as 9*

- *6.000 is presented as 6*

- *2.00 is presented as 2*

JavaScript and other computer programming languages are based on the IEEE 754 standard, or the Standard for Floating-Point Arithmetic.

Number literals can be a floating-point number, an integer or a hexadecimal.

Example of floating-point numbers:

- *4.516*

- *9.134*

- *6.01*

- *4.121*

Examples of integers:

- *34*

- *45*

- *21*

- *30*

Examples of hexadecimal numbers

- OxFF

- -OxCCFF

Special number values

- **'NaN' and 'Infinity'** - are JavaScript's two 'error values'

  The NaN (Not a Number) error appears when the browser cannot parse the number, or when an operation failed.

On the other hand, Infinity is an error that appears when the number cannot be represented because of its magnitude. The error also appears when you divide a number by zero (0).

- **-0 and +0** – the -0 rarely appears, so don't get confused about these special number values. You can ignore them, for now.

- **Null** – these are obtained when the browser cannot return a value.

2. Strings

Strings are data types that are typically enclosed in matching single quotes or double quotes. The elements can be numbers or texts.

Strings are discussed more on chapters 13 to 21.

3. Boolean

These data types represent either 'true' or 'false'. Through the use of Boolean, you can find out whether a JavaScript expression is 'true' or 'false'.

The 'true' returns are generally obtained from expressions with true values, such as number equations and similar expressions.

In contrast, 'false' returns are obtained from expressions without true values.

Example 1:

(3 > 9)

Of course, this is false because 9 is definitely greater than 3.

Example 2:

(2<3)

Obviously, the statement is 'true'. There's no need for an explanation on that one.

Example 3:

(4=9)

A 'ReferenceError' will occurre on the third example. This is because in JavaScript language, and most computer programming language, the equal sign (=) is not a symbol of equality. The equal sign is used in assigning the values or elements of variables.

See next image:

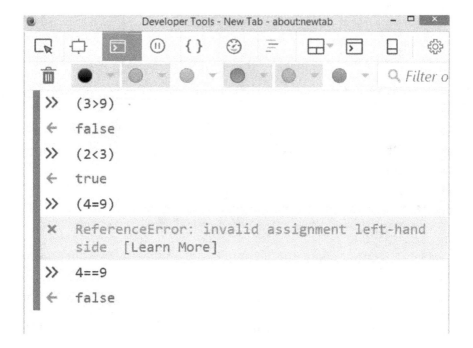

Hence, the correct sign/symbol to use should be == or === (refer to chapters 22 to 23, about Math Expressions.)

When the correct JavaScript syntax was utilized, the expression returned with a 'false' value because even with the correct sign, 4 is still not equal to 9.

4. Objects

Objects encompass all data types in the sense that numbers, Booleans, and strings can be objects. Data, such as arrays, regular expressions, dates and math are objects, as well

Objects contain many values and have properties (name:values pair) and methods (process or action). Thus, they are containers of named values. This name:values pair is called property (name) and property values (values).

They can be a collection of various different data.

Examples:

- *student: "Johnson"*

- *country: "Sweden"*

- *street: "Reed Avenue"*

Example:

var students = {firstName: "Lena", lastName: "Dean"};

See image below:

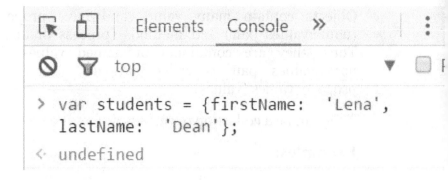

```
> var students = {firstName:   'Lena',
    lastName:   'Dean'};
< undefined
```

They are typically expressed in pairs as 'name:value'.
Take note of the colon in between the pair, and the
commas after each pair. The property values are in
quotes, and the entire statement is in brackets.

You can understand more about objects in the next
chapter, and the chapters about arrays. Since the data types of
variables are discussed in the various chapters, you'll come to
understand more about variables as you discover their vital
role in JavaScript coding.

Chapter 11: Using Prototypes

You will sometimes hear scripters talk about Prototypes in JavaScript, and you may be wondering what they are. Read on.

What are JavaScript Prototypes?

Before you could understand Prototypes, you have to understand 'objects'. In the previous chapter, you have read about objects and how they contain properties, methods, how they work, and how they are created.

Together with extensible attributes and class, prototypes are one of the attributes of objects,

As mentioned, you can create objects using the name:"values" pair. Let's create an object on students:

Example 1:

var student1 = {firstName: "Daniel", lastName: "Johnson", gender: "male"};

Example 2:

Var student2 = Object.create(new Object());

student2.firstName = 'Daniel";

71

student2.lastName = 'Johnson';

student2.gender = 'male';

```
Developer Tools - New Tab - about:newtab
Insp...  Co...  Debu...  { } Style E...  Ca...  Perform...  Net...  < > ...
Net      CSS      JS      Security    Logging    Server

>> var student1 = {firstName: 'Daniel', lastName: 'Johnson', gender: 'male'};
<- undefined
>> var student2 = Object.create(new Object());
<- undefined
>> student1.firstName = 'Daniel';
<- "Daniel"
>> student2.firstName = 'Daniel'
<- "Daniel"
>> student2.lastName = 'Johnson';
<- "Johnson"
>> student2.gender = 'male';
```

Now, in the next example, the 'function student' is called, using the following program/code/statements.

function student(lastName, gender) {

  this.lastname = lastName;

  this.gender = gender;

}

student.prototype.gender = "male";

"male"

var student3 = new student("lastName", "gender");

As you can see, the function student is like calling the functions of the first student.

Functions and objects have Prototype properties, although they are used differently, they are still crucial parts of JavaScript coding.

Functions can be constructors and non-constructors, nevertheless, they still have Prototypes.

Two general types of prototypes

1. Prototypes of functions (Prototype property)

These Prototypes can create new objects, as a function constructor, based on the object's instance. Keep in mind that the Prototype property is empty by default.

It's called the Prototype-based inheritance too, because it inherits properties from the parent Prototype function.

2. Prototypes of objects (Prototype attribute)

These Prototypes are object instances from which the objects have inherited from.

That means that every object has a 'parent' object that it inherited its attributes from.

Hence, it accesses properties of objects. The parent object is contained in the ___pro___'pseudo' property.

The objects have all properties 'inherited' from the Object.prototype.

Here are examples, so you can understand better.

function Apparel () {

this.store = "Walden";

this.isFashion = true;

}

See next image:

Apparel.prototype.showNameAndColor = function () {

console.log("Walk the ramp with me," + this.name + " and my color is " + this.store);

}

See image below:

```
> Apparel.prototype.showNameAndColor =
  function () {
  console.log('Walk the ramp with me,' +
  this.name + ' and my color is ' +
  this.store);
  }
< function () {
  console.log('Walk the ramp with me,' +
  this.name + ' and my color is ' +
  this.store);
  }
```

    I know this may seem complex, but look at it this way; it's like coming up with a function Prototype from an object Prototype. The last Prototype created a new object from the 'parent' Prototype (the first function – function Apparel), after a series of processes.

    Notice the process of adding properties, such as name and color.

A simpler example is this:

function Apparel (type) {

this.type = type;

}

This is the parent function, from which your Prototype will come from.

See image below:

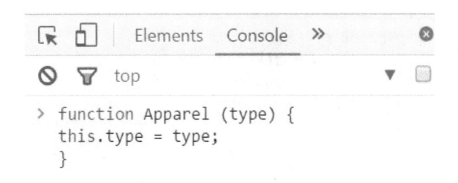

As we have said, every function has a Prototype property and the function Apparel has one too.

Let's try adding properties to the function property of apparel. The property that we have added is 'fashionable'.

When we create a new variable, 'cotton', the new variable is equivalent == to the Apparel Prototype.

That was why when the statement was executed ('Enter' key was pressed), it has returned the value 'true'.

This means that cotton is also 'fashionable', which is the property of the Apparel Prototype.

The new variable (cotton) has inherited the property of the 'parent' function and the Apparel Prototype.

Apparel.prototype.fashionable = 'apparel';

"apparel"

var cotton = new Apparel('cotton');

undefined

cotton.__proto__ == Apparel.prototype

true

Note: The purple letters are the return values when 'Enter' was pressed. This true with all of the codes. The return values are included in some of the JavaScript statements, so look out for them.

See image below:

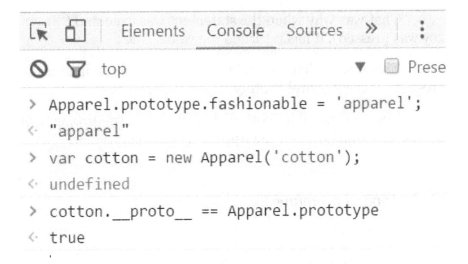

Hopefully, this will help you understand the functions of Prototypes.

Reminders:

- In JavaScript, all functions have prototypes.

- The word __proto__ is composed of TWO underscore symbols__ + proto + TWO underscore symbols __

- Because of Prototypes, a user can now have access to the properties of the variables.

Chapter 12: Program Flow Controls

JavaScript has its own organized program flow. The order in which statements are executed, typically starts from the top of the program/script/code going downwards. BUT – this is when there are no other actions/commands that the first statement has to execute.

For example, with the function 'prompt', the browser has to wait for the user to interact with the prompt, before it could proceed to the next command.

Primarily the functions control the flow of the program. Some of the functions may divert the flow to various directions. One function can lead to another function that could slow down the flow.

In this statement:

var myString = '12345678';

var length = myString.length;

document.write('This is the length of my string: ' + length);

The program flow could be:

- Input the new variable

- Measure the length of the string.

- Write return value of "This is the length of my string..." on the screen.

The flow in this statement is organized, but you have also to consider how fast or slow your browser is.

The flow controls control the flow of the JavaScript program. There are two types of flow controls:

1. **Loop types**

   These are indicated by iteration, repetition or continuity of the action or execution of the code. It makes use of for, for-in, while, do-while. This is discussed in chapter 32, on the topic about loops.

   Likewise, 'break' and 'continue' for loops can affect the program flow. Break stops the loop and terminate it, while continue allows the loop to resume its action.

   Example:

   for (number=0;number<10;number++)

if   (number==6)   break;   else
document.write(number+'<br>');

See image below:

If you view the image above, the loop is broken, and the return value only showed numbers 0 to 5 on the screen.

If you insert this in an HTML code, you can use this code:

<html>

<head>

<script>

for (number=0;number<10;number++)

if   (number==6)   break;   else
document.write(number+'<br>');

81

```
</script>

</head>

</html>
```

See image below:

```
File  Edit  Format  View  Help
<html>
<head>
<title>Break</title>
<script>
for (number=0;number<10;number++)
if (number==6) break; else document.write(number+'<br>');
</script>
</head>
</html>
```

2. Decision types

In this type, the program flows according to a condition. These statements make use of conditions, such as 'if', 'else-if', for/in, while/do while, and similar statements.

'if' statements are the simplest condition statement.

Example:

if (condition) {

statement

}

There are examples of condition statements in chapters 27 to 28, for the decision type statements.

The difference between loops and decision type flow controls is that loops has a continuous action unless broken, while decision flow controls execute only the command once.

Chapter 13: Creating Strings

What are strings and what are their functions in JavaScript? We'll have to learn first about strings in this chapter because they are significant parts of your JavaScript codes.

What is a string?

A string is a word, or a group of words or texts that 1s/are enclosed inside a single quotation mark (' ') or double quotation marks (" "). You can store them by identifying them as variables with the keyword 'var'.

Examples: The examples are presented in italics, so you can identify them immediately.

- *alert ("My name is Jekyll.")*

    The string in this example is = "*My name is Jekyll.*"

- *var name = "Jekyll"*

    In the second example, the string is "*Jekyll*".

Take note that the double quotes may be replaced by a single quote and still be called a 'string'.

Examples: Using the same examples, we come up with examples of single quotes:

- *alert ('My name is Jekyll. ')*

The string in this example is = 'My name is Jekyll.'

- *var name = 'Jekyll'*

In the second example, the string is 'Jekyll'.

Uses of String:

1. **A string can create alerts with the keyword 'alert'.**

Example:

alert ('Hello, enjoy your stay here.")

Take note:

The 'alert' is usually a pop-up for users to read. You can now use your Mozilla or Google Chrome 'Console' to test whether your codes work or not.

You may want to 'clear' your previous entries, by pressing the ⊘ symbol, found on the left upper portion of your console.

In your 'Console', type 'alert' ("Hello, enjoy your stay here."). See the example above. After you press 'enter'. The pop-up or alert will appear with the string you have typed.

Some programmers use the keyword 'window.alert'. For this book, we will use the simple form - 'alert'.

See image below:

2. You can cut your strings and combine them to create new ones.

The old strings are not deleted, but you can create a new one out of the previous strings.

Example:

You have these two strings: Try typing them on your Google Chrome console:

mystring1 = "My name is Jekyll."

mystring2 = "I am twenty years old."

See image below:

You want to combine your strings, specifically the words "Jekyll" and "twenty years old"

Your code would be:

alert ("Jekyll,"+ " twenty years old.");

After you press 'Enter', the alert will pop-up.

See image below:

3. **You can create two alerts in one line**.

   Just separate the first alert with a semicolon to indicate that it has ended, and that you're creating a new one:

   Example:

   alert ('Good morning!'); alert ('How are you today?');

   See image below:

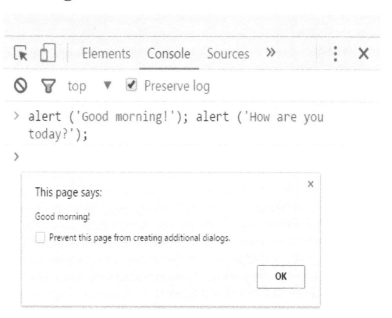

In the Mozilla 'Console', the alert will appear this way:

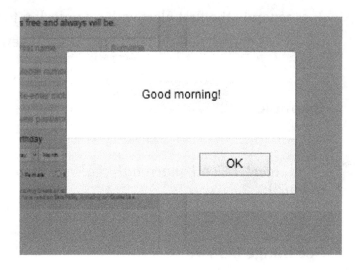

After you have pressed 'OK', the second alert will appear.

For Chrome, see image below:

This page says:

How are you today?

☐ Prevent this page from creating additional dialogs.

OK

For Mozilla:

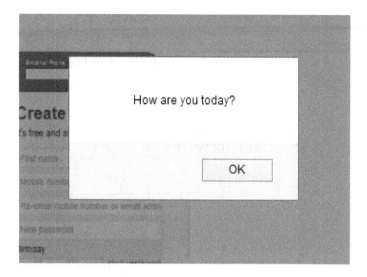

Reminders:

- Enclose your word-strings with matching double quotes or single quotes.

- Add a space before the word - if there are words before it in the old string, and add a space after the word, if there are words after it in the old string.

- add the semicolon to indicate that the statement/command/code has ended.

- In some browsers, when you have to add words with quotes in them, use the backslash \ before the single quote, or for double quotes before the word, and before the closing double quotes.

Example 1:

var message1 = "I don't want to come.";

Whether you create the code like the sample statement above, or you write the statement like the sample statement below, Mozilla and Google Chrome will execute them anyhow, and produce correct results/return data.

var message1 = "I don\'t want to come.";

Example 2

var message2 = "Never mention the "neopoliticians" because this is

dangerous.";

In some browsers, to create the code correctly for the above statement, write your code this way:

var messge2 = "Never mention the \"neopoliticians\" because this

is dangerous. ";

See next image: The slash is not displayed.

- The backslash \ can also be used to break up a code line within a text string. However, you cannot break up a code line using the same symbol.

- Not all browsers recognize this symbol, though, so you may want to use the plus sign (+) to add your strings.

  Example:

  alert('I am excited to learn about JavaScript.\ It is so interesting.');

See next image:

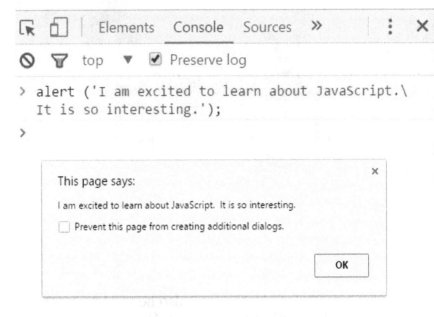

Reminders:

- You don't need the backslash in your Chrome and Mozilla for JavaScript, because the browser will execute the code of the string, even with the quotes within the texts.

- The backslash is more commonly used to comment on JavaScript codes and to block the execution of a code.

Chapter 14: Finding and Replacing Strings

You can find a string and replace it, if you want to. You just have to use the correct method. The keyword for this procedure is:

string.replace(searchvalue, newvalue).

Example:

var str = 'He went to Okinawa yesterday. ';

var set = str.replace (/Okinawa/g, 'Seoul');

```
str = 'He went to Okinawa yesterday.'
set = str.replace(/Okinawa/g, 'Seoul');
"He went to Seoul yesterday."
```

Notice that 'Okinawa' was replace by 'Seoul'. The small 'g' after the replacement word stands for 'global'.

The browser could either be locale or global. It's recommended to use global, to prevent errors.

You can return the replacement text or word by using the 'function' and 'return' keywords.

Chapter 15: Concatenating Strings

You can concatenate (combine) strings, or parts of strings with each other. You can concatenate strings by using the plus (+) operator. Let's say you have this original alert statement:

"My name is Jekyll.";

See image below:

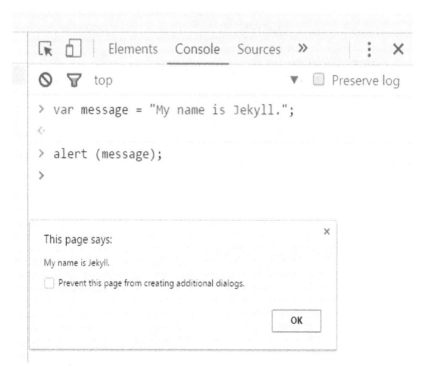

Consequently, you want to concatenate another string and add the input of the user (about her user name) on your website. You can create another variable for this. using another code.

userName = "Susan";

So, if you want to combine the message and the userName in your alert, you can write the JavaScript this way:

message = "My name is Jekyll";

userName = "Jean";

alert ("My name is " + userName);

Keep in mind that when you press 'Enter' on the console your input will appear just below your script, and at the end, the alert box will pop-up because you have created an alert.

See image below:

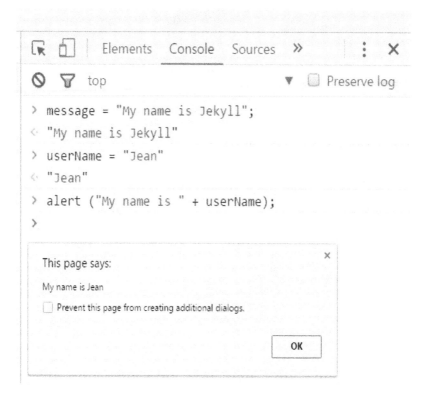

Notice that there's a space before the closing double quotes in the code. This will allow the correct combination of the two strings. If you don't leave a space, your resulting alert will appear this way. *"My name isJean."*

See image below:

```
> alert ("My name is" + userName);
>
```

This page says:

My name isJean

☐ Prevent this page from creating additional dialogs.

OK

Browsers can run JavaScript in their own way, so be able to adjust accordingly.

Chapter 16: Measuring Strings

In JavaScript, you can also measure the length of the strings just like the other programming language. It's easy to perform this task by using two methods.

Measuring a string

Developers and programmers may want to measure the length of the string, so that they could allow the web user to interact and input his data properly.

As a new scripter, you can learn this task too.

For example, if you're asking the user to input his name in your prompt, you have to specify the length of characters that the user is allowed to input. You can measure the length of the string by using this code/statement:

var length = myString.length;

Example:

var myString = '12345678';

var length = myString.length;

document.write('This is the length of my string: ' + length);*

See next image:

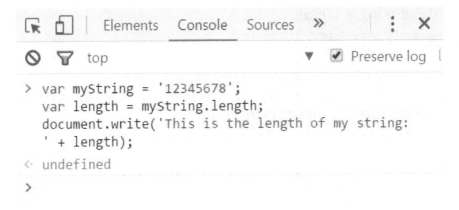

Result: This will appear on your browser.

This is the length of my string: 8

If you are to insert this script in your website's HTML, this is how the JavaScript code will appear:

```
<script>

var myString = '12345678';

var length = myString.length;

document.write('This is the length of my string:    ' +
length);

</script>
```

You can insert this js.script in the <head> or <body> portion of your HTML.

You may also write the code this way:

```
<script type = "text/javascript">

var myString = "12345678";

var length = myString.length;

document.write('This is the length of my string:    " +
length);

</script>
```

- Take note of the opening and closing script tags.

As you gain more inserting your scripts into HTML and CSS, you will also learn these markup languages slowly.

You don't have to pressure yourself to do so, they are slowly being introduced in this book, simply to help you with your JavaScript codes' insertion.

Chapter 17: Slicing and Extracting Strings

You can slice the characters of your string and extract characters you want. Yup, just like you slice your meat and food.

This is relatively easy with the keyword:

str.slice(start, end);

The extracted characters will appear in your return values.

Example 1:

str = 'It is my first time to use JavaScript.';

res = str.slice(2,6);

" is " // This is the result of your code/command.

Example 2:

str = 'It is my first time to use JavaScript.';

res = str.slice(1,4);

"t i"   //This is the result of the second JavaScript statement.

See next image: This is from Mozilla console:

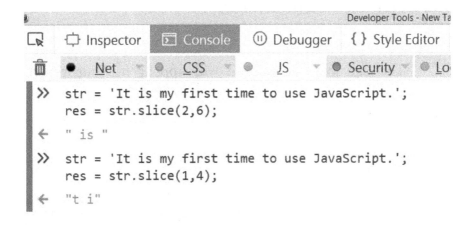

This is from your Chrome 'Console'. Both browsers returned the same results:

```
> str = 'It is my first time to use JavaScript.';
  res = str.slice(2,6);
< " is "
>
```

Remember that the string character length starts with 0, and then 1, 2, and so on.

Therefore, in this example, if you wanted to extract the string starting from 2 and then up to 6, your end value should be 7.

The result will show only up to character 5. Take note that the extracted substring is only up to 5 and doesn't include 6.

If you want to show substrings up to 6 in the result, you will have to change your statement to:

str = 'It is my first time to use JavaScript.';

res = str.slice(2,7);

So, how come the result was " is " for the code: res = str.slice(2,6)?

This is because the positions assigned to the string are these: (from 2 – 5)

Assigned positions:

I =0

t =1

blank space=2 /this is where you wanted to start slicing.

i=3

s =4

blank space=5   //this is where you wanted to end your slice. Thus your result was " is " (blank space, 'is', and another blank space.)

m =6 //this is not included; it's used to indicate the end of the slice.

y =7

space = 8

t =9

i=10

m=11

e=11

space = 12

… and so on. Hopefully, you got the drift.

Don't worry, you will get used to these JavaScript syntax as you continue to learn.

For example 2:

str = 'It is my first time to use JavaScript.';

res = str.slice(1,4);

The positions assigned are the same; only the 'end' has changed. In the code above, it indicates that the start would be substring/position 1 and the end would be substring/position 3.

The result was:

res = "t i"

How come this was the result?

Observe the assigned positions of the characters below. It's similar to the first example. Only this time, the end of the slice is 4. So, the result will show you 1 to 3.

I = 0

t = 1   //this is where you wanted to start slicing.

blank space = 2

i=3   //this is where you wanted to end your slice.

s =4

blank space=5

m =6

y =7

space = 8

...and so forth.

Going over the assigned positions, you will notice that position 1 is equivalent to "t" and the characters between 1 to 3 are: a blank space and then 'i'.

Thus, the result extracted was:

res = 't i"

Indicating the end of the slice can be optional if you want to slice all the rest of the characters.

Let's say you want to extract the characters starting from 4 up to the end of the string. This would be your code:

str = 'It is my first time to use JavaScript.';

res = str.slice(4);

The result would show the 4th character and all the rest of the characters in the string.

If you go back to the positions of the characters that we have discussed previously, "s" is index 4.

Therefore, you will be extracting from "s" and up to the end of the string. Thus, the result is:

"s my first time to use JavaScript."

See next image:

To extract only the first character of your string, you can use this code:

str = 'It is my first time to use JavaScript.';

res = str.slice(0, 1);

The result will be this:

'I".

See image below: This is from Mozilla.

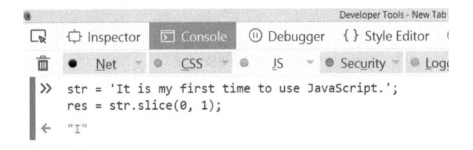

If you want to extract the whole string, use these keywords:

res = str.slice(0);

Hence, your final code would be:

str = 'It is my first time to use JavaScript.';

res = str.slice(0);

The result will be:

"It is my first time to use JavaScript."

See image below:

Reminders:

- Again, you can use single quotes or double quotes for your strings. I have to stress this repeatedly because most of my errors were from these quotes.

  I alternated using them, because there were times, the console accepted the double quotes, but there were times it didn't.

  If you obtain errors even if your code is correct, it might be because of your quotes.

Change what you're using currently to the other type. If you're using double quotes, switch to single quotes and vice versa.

- You can both explore Mozilla and Chrome and use the browser you're most comfortable with. In this book, I'm working on both Google and Mozilla. You choose your own browser; you're the boss.

Chapter 18: Converting Strings

Learning how to convert your data to strings is an added advantage for you. The secret is knowing what keywords to use and how to write the code correctly.

The general code for this is:

String(object);

1. **Converting numbers to strings:**

var myNumber = 10;

var myString = myNumber.toString();

Although, the keyword 'var' was not used in the code below, the browser (Chrome) was still able to recognize the script. The problem is, the data cannot be stored.

See image below:

```
  ⟨ₖ  ⟨⟩  │  Elements   Console   Sources   »   ⋮   ✕

  ⊘  ▽  top                              ▼  ☑ Preserve log

  >  myNumber = 10;
  ⟨·  10
  >  myString = myNumber.toString();
  ⟨·  "10"
  >  |
```

You can also use this code:

> *myNumber = 10;*
>
> *myString = String(myNumber);*

These two codes will give you the same results - "10".

2. **Converting a string to lowercase or uppercase:**

Yes, you can do that quickly with the correct code.

Example:

> *var myString1 = "I enjoy writing my JavaScript codes. ";*
>
> *var myString2 = myString1.toUpperCase();*

```
Inspector    Console    Debugger    { } Style Editor
   Net         CSS         JS        Security    Lo

>>  myString1 = 'I enjoy writing my JavaScript codes.';
<-  "I enjoy writing my JavaScript codes."
>>  myString2 = myString1.toUpperCase();
<-  "I ENJOY WRITING MY JAVASCRIPT CODES."
```

You can also convert the string to a LocaleUpperCase by using this statement:

myString3 = myString1.toLocaleUpperCase();

See image below (last line):

When uncertain about the JavaScript capability of 'Locale' browsers, it's wiser to use the non-locale. This is due to the fact that the statement's Unicode may work differently in the case mappings of the 'Locale' browser. But when both work correctly, you will be obtaining the same results, like the example above.

By the way, when you assign the values of your variables, you may not use the keyword 'var'. This is because Mozilla and Chrome can recognize the entries without the 'var' keyword before the variable name. See image above.

However, if you want to save your data, then you have to name them as variables and use the keyword 'var'.

Each time you press 'Enter', the output will already be displayed, so you just have to type your next statement after the result appears on your screen.

3. Converting a string to the lowercase

Example: You can write each statement, one at a time, and observe if the results are correct.

myString1 = 'I enjoy writing my JavaScript codes.';

myString2 = myString1.toLowerCase();

myString3 = myString1.toLocaleLowerCase();

Converting a string to the lowercase is similar to converting it to the uppercase. All you have to do is to change the keyword.

Here are the images of the statements in the example above. For the first statement: The result is the brown-colored words.

For the second statement: myString2 = myString1.toLowerCase(); Here's the result, when 'Enter' is pressed on the 'Console'.

"i enjoy writing my javascript codes."

All the capitalized letters were converted to lowercase.

See next image:

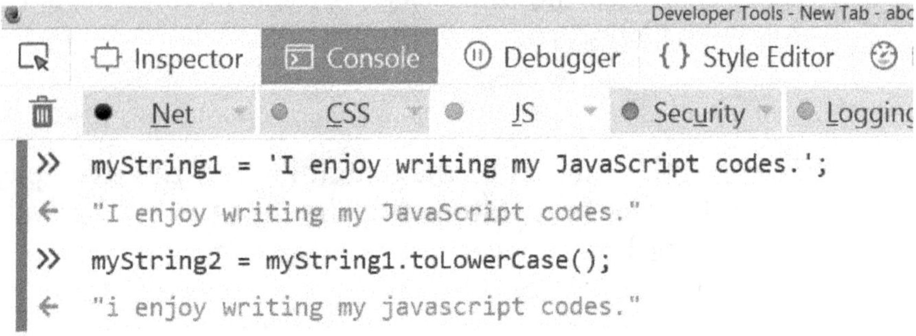

```
>>  myString1 = 'I enjoy writing my JavaScript codes.';
←   "I enjoy writing my JavaScript codes."
>>  myString2 = myString1.toLowerCase();
←   "i enjoy writing my javascript codes."
```

When the 'Locale' is used, it produced the same results:

"i enjoy writing my javascript codes."

See image below: (5th and 6th line)

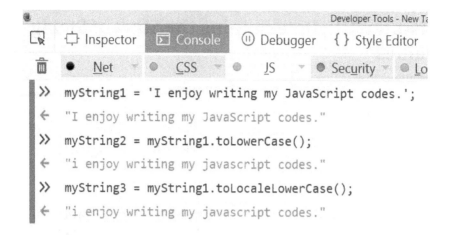

These simple instructions may seem trivial to advance programmers, but for beginners, I know how difficult it can be for you. It's like learning how to walk before you can even crawl. So, I presented it in a simple manner.

But, cheer up! You can learn more, if you continue to persist and persevere.

Chapter 19: Determining the Start of String Values

The most common string methods were explained in the previous chapters. Here are other methods that you may need, when you write your JavaScript codes.

1. **startsWith()** – the function of this is to determine if the string starts with the indicated characters. If it does, the result will show 'true'. If it does not the result will show 'false'.

   Let's say you want to determine if the string starts with an "I", you can write the JavaScript this way:

   Example:

   var res = myString1.startsWith ('I'); or str.startsWith (I);

   Since I have previously assigned the values of my string earlier in the code, which is, *myString1 = 'I enjoy writing my JavaScript codes.'*, so, I was able to obtain the result promptly.

   See image below: (from Mozilla)

```
>>  res = myString1.startsWith('I');
←   true
```

Notice also that just like the previous example, the keyword 'var' was not used in the codes. They were not saved, so there was no problem about that.

But I included the keyword 'var' in these examples because your browser may need it.

If you used it, and the browser returns an error, then you can remove it. Part of learning is committing mistakes and learning from them, right?

Now, let's have another example.

var res = myString1.startsWith('M');

See image below:

```
[icons] | Elements   Console   Sources   »   ⋮   ✕
⊘ ▼  top                              ▼  ☐ Preserve log
> res = myString1.startsWith('M');
< false
>
```

The result obtained was 'false', based on the values of myString1, which is, *'I enjoy writing my JavaScript codes.'*

Take note that you can also write the code this way.

var res = str.startsWith();

Example: (from Chrome)

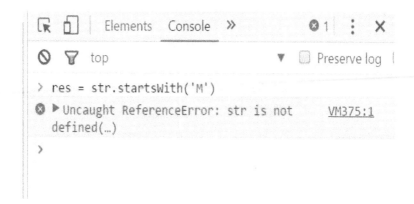

In the above image, I obtained an error return because my 'str' was not defined.

If this happens to you, then you have to assign a value to your string first.

Let's say you assigned this value to your string.

var str = 'It is wonderful to be alive!';

You have to input it on your 'Console', so you, or the user can use it later on.

See next image:

```
⌖  ⬚  │  Elements   Console   Sources   »       ⋮   ✕

🚫  ▼  top                            ▼  ☐ Preserve log

>  str = 'It is wonderful to be alive!';
<  "It is wonderful to be alive!"
>
```

You, or the user can now utilize it for the res =
str.startsWith(); method.

Example:

> *var str = 'It is wonderful to be alive!';*

This will return:

> *"It is wonderful to be alive!"*

> *var res= str.startsWith('M');*

This will return:

> *false*

> *var res = str.startsWith('I');*

This will return:

true

See next image:

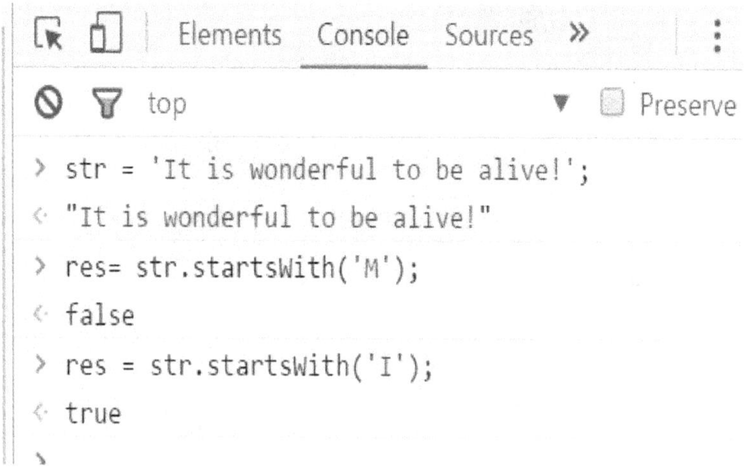

```
Elements   Console   Sources   »           ⋮

⃠  ▽  top                          ▼  ☐ Preserve

> str = 'It is wonderful to be alive!';
<  "It is wonderful to be alive!"
> res= str.startsWith('M');
<  false
> res = str.startsWith('I');
<  true
>
```

The statement could also be stated this way:

> *var res = string.startsWith(searchValue, start);*

Where:

searchValue is the indicated character/string to search for

start = indicates the position from where to start the search. This is optional and may be omitted if you want to search the entire string.

Example 1:

var res = str.startsWith ('I',4);

The Boolean result is:

false

This is because the 'str' values (*'It is wonderful to be alive!'*), starting at position 4, does not start with 'I'. Note: position 4 starts with 's'.

Example 2:

var res = str.startsWith('is'', 3);

See image below:

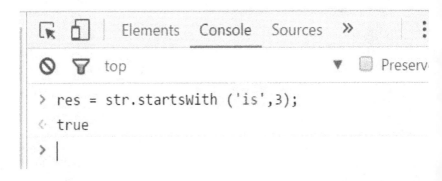

The return is 'true' because 'is' is the 3rd value in the string.

Remember that if the start value is not indicated, the whole string will be included in the Boolean (true or false) return.

Chapter 20: Searching for a String

You can search for a regular expression, or an indicated value in a string using the statement:

search() or string.search(searchValue)

This will return the position of the indicated value. The search value will be a regular expression (RegExp).

Example:

var myString1 = 'I enjoy writing my JavaScript codes. ';

var res = myString1.search('my);

Let's use the same values from the previous examples, and input it:

Let's now use our search statement"

var res = myString1.search('my');

The result is 16.

See image below:

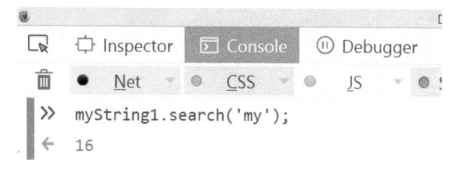

This is because the position of 'my' in the string is in index 16. Remember to start counting from 0, and include blank spaces.

Example 2:

> *var str = 'It is wonderful to be alive!';*
>
> *var res = str.search('a');*

The result would be 22, indicating the position of the specified character.

See next image:

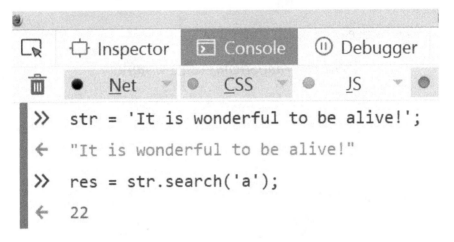

Reminders:

- Strings can be anything, from numbers to texts.

- The string values have to be assigned first before you can perform the commands.

- In this example, I have written the statements one by one and pressed 'Enter', so the results (brown-colored words, and blue numbers) appeared in between the JavaScript statements in the image.

- You could also use string.search(); as long as you have defined your string.

- If no match is identified, the result will return a value of (-1).

- Just in case you haven't noticed: the writing space for Mozilla is found at the bottom part of the 'Console'. It's a small strip of white space with two arrows >> that indicate where you should start typing.

- Chrome has the whole 'Console' for you to type in.

- If the search is case-sensitive, indicate it in the code with the letter 'i'.

Example:

var res = myString1.search(/my/i);

This will return the value 16.

See image below:

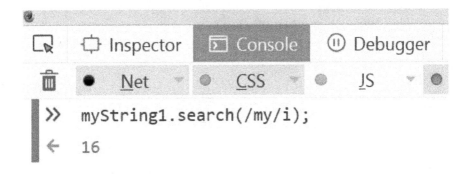

As previously mentioned, the string, myString1, has assigned values already, that was why the browser did not return an error.

Chapter 21: Repeating Strings

Strings can be repeated, as often as you want, using the correct JavaScript statement/code.

You can do this by using this syntax:

string.repeat(count) or str.repeat(count)

Where:

Count is the number of times you want the old string repeated in the new string. Keep in mind that your old string still exists and that you're creating a new string.

Example:

var myString1 = 'I enjoy writing my JavaScript codes. ';

var res = myString1.repeat(5);

See image below: for Mozilla

```
>>   res = myString1.repeat(5);
←    "I enjoy writing my JavaScript codes.I enjoy
     writing my JavaScript codes.I enjoy writing
     my JavaScript codes.I enjoy writing my
     JavaScript codes.I enjoy writing my
     JavaScript codes."
```

You will be obtaining the same results from Chrome: I have assigned values in Chrome for myString1 because it returns an error that myString1 was not defined.

Notice that you can use the name of your string, but it must be specified in your repeat command. When I used:

res = string.repeat(5);

I obtained a return error because the string was not defined.

See next image:

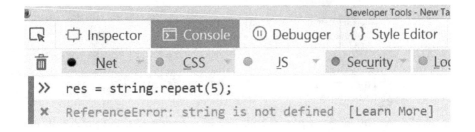

Let's try to define the string and see what happens.

Example:

> *var string = "Love can move mountains.";*

When you execute the command:

> *var res = string.repeat(5);*

The 'Console' will execute it with the expected output – the string is repeated 5 times.

See next image:

Is it going well for you so far?

Hopefully, you can appreciate the simple presentation.

For advance scripters, these all may seem 'boring', but it's crucial for beginners to understand the basics, so if you're reading this book. You will have to endure.

Chapter 22: JavaScript and Math Operators

There are common operators that you can use in JavaScript. Don't worry, the most common, or the basic operators, are those that you're familiar with since grade school.

Basic operators

- + for addition of numbers, and for strings – acts as a concatenation operator

- * for multiplication

- - for subtraction

- / for division

- % for remainder - This is a modulus operator. It will give the remainder of the answer, and not the answer to the division. When the number can be divided evenly by another number, it returns the value 0.

- ++ increment – this increases the integer value by one, incrementally.

- -- decrement – this decreases the integer value by one, decrementally.

Your JavaScript console can act as your calculator too. JavaScript observes mathematical expressions, recognizing the symbols in the expressions. Values are the numbers in your expressions. You can save your expressions by referencing it using letters.

Examples for addition:

Type 6 + 4 on your console, when you press 'Enter', the answer, which is 10, will appear.

Type 1234 + 4567 on your console, when you press 'Enter', the answer, which is 5801, will appear.

See image below:

Examples for multiplication:

Type 723 * 137 on your 'Console' and press 'Enter', the answer 99051 will appear.

Type 3190 * 287 on your 'Console' and press 'Enter', the answer 915530, will appear.

See image below:

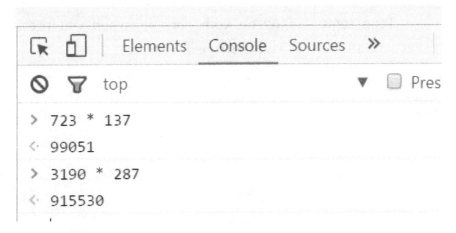

Examples for subtraction and multiplication:

See next image:

You can also compute for complex expressions:

Examples:

$$(456 + 786) / (235 - 123) = 11.089285714285714$$

Example:

$$[(456 * 786) + (235 - 134)]/3 = 119505.666666666667$$

See image below:

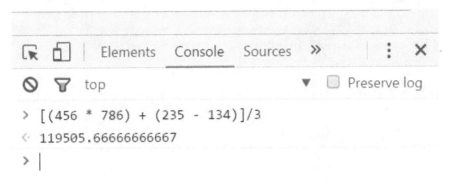

In the above-mentioned problem, since (456*786) and (235-134) are enclosed in parentheses, they are solved first. This is followed by addition of the answers of both expressions inside the parentheses.

Then, lastly, is the division of the final answer (all values enclosed inside the brackets) by 3. This will give you the final answer: 119505.66666666667

The JavaScript 'Console' will solve the problem chronologically using the common math order, PEMDAS (Parentheses, Exponents, Multiplication, Division, Addition and then Subtraction). This denotes the order in which the browser/console computes for the math or algebraic expression.

Hence, it will solve the numbers/values inside the parentheses first. If there are no parenthesis, it will solve the exponents next, then the multiplication, followed by the division, then addition and lastly subtraction.

You can indicate which calculation you want JavaScript to solve first by enclosing them in parentheses. If you don't specify, JavaScript will apply the PEMDAS method of computing the values.

I won't elaborate more on this because I presume that you remember your basic mathematics and algebra.

Now, the wonderful thing about JavaScript is that you can add numbers to variables, or add the variables only, and still get a number, as an answer.

When errors occur in your JavaScript, red letters will appear indicating what error/s you have committed.

JavaScript does not require you to convert the terms into similar terms, as long as the variables have been assigned and defined correctly. For 6 + 4 = 10, you can also do these:

Examples:

commonNumber = 6;

commonNumber + 4;

See image below:

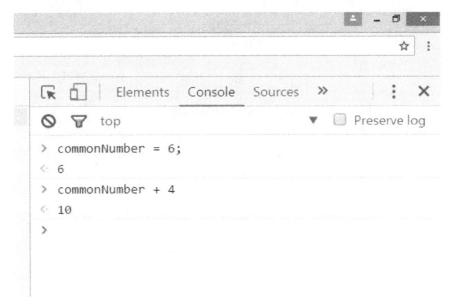

If you noticed, the second statement: commonNumber + 4, doesn't have a semicolon after it, but still, JavaScript has computed it.

Other programmers express the statement as:

var commonNumber = 6;

var commonNumber + 4;

The above statement will give you the same answer - 10. You have added a variable and a number, and still obtained the answer 10.

You can also add the variables, without using the numbers and still get the same answer. You can play with the variables anyway you want.

As soon as you press 'Enter' the JavaScript console will give you the answer. It's more awesome than a calculator.

Examples:

commonNumber = 6;

anotherNumber = 4;

finalNumber = commonNumber + anotherNumber;

anotherNumber = finalNumber – commonNumber;

See next image:

```
    ⋮    ⟨ ◻    Elements   Console   Sources  »       ⋮   ✕

    ⊘  ▽  top                              ▼  ◻ Preserve log
  > commonNumber = 6;
  ⟨· 6
  > commonNumber + 4
  ⟨· 10
  > anotherNumber = 4;
  ⟨· 4
  > finalNumber = commonNumber + anotherNumber;
  ⟨· 10
  > anotherNumber = finalNumber - commonNumber;
  ⟨· 4
  >
```

Other programmers may express the statement above as
follows:

> *var commonNumber = 6;*

> *var anotherNumber = 4;*

> *var finalNumber = var commonNumber + var*
anotherNumber;

> *var anotherNumber = var finalNumber –*
commonNumber;

You can also turn your statements into alerts.

Example:

alert(commonNumber + anotherNumber);

or *alert(6+)*

See image below:

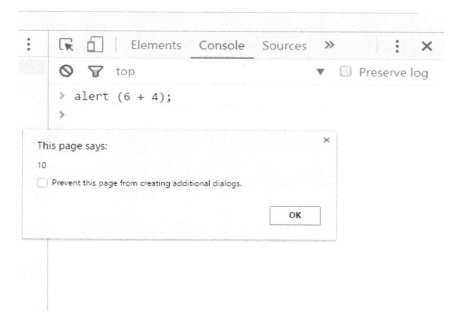

Don't forget that numbers can be viewed as strings, if they are enclosed in matching quotes; hence, they will be treated as strings during the execution of a statement.

Chapter 23: Other Operators Use in Math Expressions

There are other math operators included in your JavaScript that you must know about.

1. **Making use of the ++ sign.**

    num++; is the same as *num = num + 1;*

    The ++ sign denotes increments of 1 is added to the variable

    See image below:

```
:      [R  [] |  Elements  Console  Sources  »       :   X

       🚫  🝙  top                          ▼  ☐  Preserve log

   >  num = 5;

   <·  5

   >  num = num + 1;

   <·  6

   >  num++;

   <·  6

   >  num++;

   <·  7

   >  num++;

   <·  8

   >  |
```

2. Making use of the num- -

This is the opposite of num++. It subtracts increment of 1 from the value of the variable.

See image below:

```
R  □  |  Elements  Console  Sources  »       ⋮  X
◯  ▽  top                              ▼  ☐ Preserve log

>  num = 5;
<· 5
>  num--;
<· 5
>  num--;
<· 4
>  num--;
<· 3
>  num--;
<· 2
>  |
```

Take note:

'Expressions' is a term applied not only to math. The term 'expressions' can also be applied to a combination of values, such as numbers and strings.

When you type numbers on your console, it will respond automatically to it, and perform the obvious computations.

If you don't want this to happen, convert your number to strings.

Assignment operators:

Operators	Example	Equivalent to
= (simple assignment)	c = a + b var name = "Don"	Variable c has assigned values of a + b
+= (add and assignment)	b+= a	b = b + a
-= (subtract and assignment	b-= a	b = b - a
/= (divide and assignment)	b/= a	b = b / a
*= (multiply and assignment)	b*= a	b = b * a
% (modules and assignment)	b % a	b = b % a

Type operators

1. **instanceof** – this operator returns true, when the object type is the object's instance.

2. **typeof** – this operator returns a variable's type.

Comparison and logical operators

1. == equal to

2. === equal value and type

3. > greater than

4. >= greater than or equal to

5. < lesser than

6. <=lesser than or equal to

7. != not equal

8. !== not equal value and type

9. ? ternary operator (conditional)

Chapter 24: Creating and Displaying Date and Time

With JavaScript, you can create and display the date and time on your page. It's important to remember that the web browser is responsible in executing the JavaScript code within the HTML.

You can create and display the date and time per millisecond in your own website as you continue to learn JavaScript and other programming language.

There are two ways that the date and time is created: string and numbers.

For creating a date object, this is the general statement:

var dateObjectName = new Date([parameters]);

Example:

var summer 2022 = new Date (April 15, 2022 12:20:00");

See image below:

If you noticed, the parameters presented above is a string on the:

month day, year hours:minutes:seconds.

These are all included in the image above. There are other ways to present the parameters, such as omitting the parameters.

Example:

var today = new Date();

This will return the day of the week, month, day, year, hours, minutes and seconds.

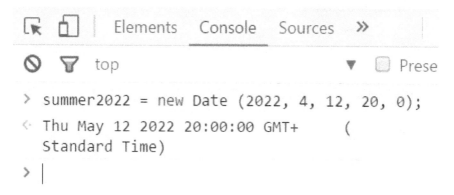

```
>  today = new Date();
<  Tue Nov 01 2016 09:04:17 GMT+      (
   Standard Time)
>
```

You can also use integers (numbers) in your parameters, by converting the date to numbers. (Year, month, day, hour, minute and seconds).

Example:

var summer2022 = new Date (2022, 4, 12, 20, 0);

See image below:

```
>  summer2022 = new Date (2022, 4, 12, 20, 0);
<  Thu May 12 2022 20:00:00 GMT+       (
   Standard Time)
>
```

Another simpler method that you can utilize as parameters is simply using the integer values of the year, month and day.

Example:

>*var summer2022 = new Date(2022, 4, 15);*

See image below:

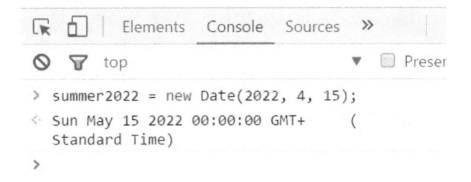

When you don't include the hours, minutes and seconds, the time will be set to zero (0).

See image below:

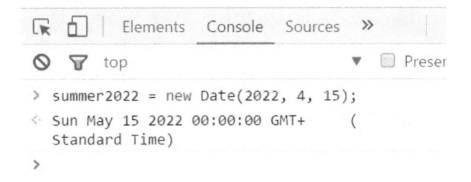

Reminders:

- If the date parameter is in word-string objects, use matching quotes (usually a double quote) to enclose the parameters.

Examples:

"March 15, 2022"

"October 20, 2018"

- For integers, there are no need for quotes.

If you're utilizing integers, take note that months have values from 0 to 11 (December is 11, while January is 0). The days of the months are 1 to 31, and the time is in milliseconds, minute and hours.

Chapter 25: Date Object Methods

Learning how to use the methods in manipulating the elements of the date and time can come in handy when you will become a full-fledged web developer and programmer. To dream is free, so why don't you dream big? After all, becoming an advance scripter starts with being a beginner.

1. 'get' method

This is used in 'getting' the values of date objects. The code for this is:

var dateObjectName.getParameter();

Example:

var summer2022.getMonth();

The return data will be = 2, because in JavaScript, March is 2.

```
[R] [i]    Elements   Console   Sources   »

⊘  ⧩  top                           ▼  ☐  Preser

>  summer2022 = new Date("March 15, 2022");
‹  Tue Mar 15 2022 00:00:00 GMT+      (
   Standard Time)
>  summer2022.getMonth;
‹  function getMonth() { [native code] }
>  summer2022.getMonth();
‹  2
⌄  |
```

I committed an error in the first 'get' code because I
omitted the parentheses. Thus, it returned the correct
function code instead.

See 2nd entry in the image above. When I corrected
the error, the 'Console' returned the correct answer,
which is 2. Keep in mind that the number of the
months start with 0.

With the 'get' method, you can obtain as many
information as you want from the date object.

The 'Console' browser provides a list as soon as you
type the function word 'get'. All you have to do is
click on them.

Here are some of the data you can obtain from 'get'.

See image below:

```
> summer2022 = new Date("March 15, 2022");
‹ Tue Mar 15 2022 00:00:00 GMT+       (        .
  Standard Time)
> summer2022.getMonth;
‹ function getMonth() { [native code] }
> summer2022.getMonth();
‹ 2
> summer2022.getFullYear();
‹ 2022
> summer2022.getDay();
‹ 2
> summer2022.getMilliseconds();
‹ 0
> summer2022.getMinutes();
‹ 0
> summer2022.getUTCFullYear();
```

2. 'set' method

This is used in setting the values of date objects. You can swiftly set the values of your date objects through this code:

var dateObjectName.setParameter();

Example:

Let's say you have created a new date object:

var newYear = ("January 1, 2017");

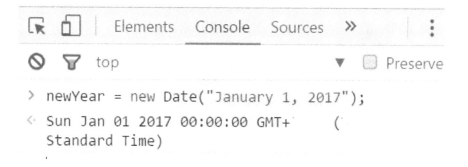

And you want to set the month, your general code would appear this way:

newYear.setMonth();

Example:

I want to set the month to February; my code would be:

newYear.setMonth(1);

This would be the return values:

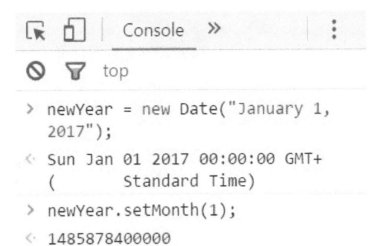

The number indicates milliseconds. One day is = 86,400,000.

After you have set the date, you can check if your input is accepted. Since the integers may be difficult to interpret, you can use the function: .

getMonth.

Example:

newYear.getMonth();

When you execute this statement, you'll get (1), which is 'February', 'January' is 0. Therefore, you have succeeded in changing the month of the date object.

See image below:

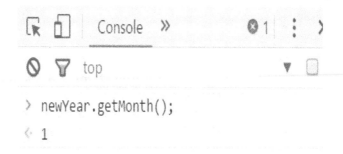

You could print it to further confirm by using the code below:

document.write(newYear);

See image below:

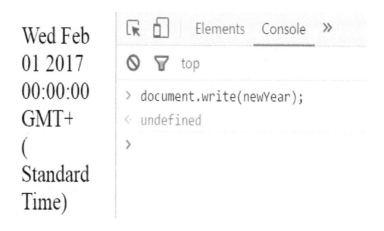

Based on the return image above, the month has indeed changed to 'February' from its original element, which is 'January'.

3. 'to' method

This is used in obtaining string values of date objects. The general code is:

var dateObjectName.toParameter();

Example:

var newYear.toDateString();

See the result or return data in the image below, when the code above was executed or ran:

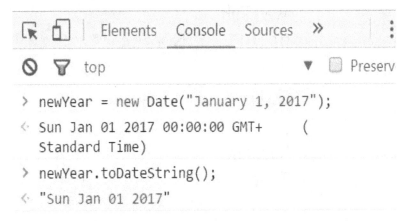

There are various 'to' methods that the 'Console' will automatically present to you when you type the keyword 'to', you can choose from those options or just continue typing the rest of your code.

Here are more 'to' commands you can do:

var newYear.toUTCString();

var newYear.toLocaleDateString();

var newYear.toGMTString();

See image below:

```
┌─┐  ┌─┐   Elements   Console   Sources   »
⊘  ▽  top                          ▼  ☐ Prese
>  newYear = new Date("January 1, 2017");
<· Sun Jan 01 2017 00:00:00 GMT+      (
   Standard Time)
>  newYear.toUTCString();
<· "Sat, 31 Dec 2016 16:00:00 GMT"
>  newYear.toLocaleDateString();
<· "1/1/2017"
>  newYear.toGMTString();
<· "Sat, 31 Dec 2016 16:00:00 GMT"
 ·  ｜
```

Don't forget to add the matching parentheses before the semicolon.

4. parse method (UTC)

This is used in parsing (analyzing) date object strings. For this, let's create a new date object.

Example:

var lastYear = new Date("October 20, 2019");

We have created lastYear as our new dateObjectName with the values "October 20, 2019".

Now, we can access the UTC, GMT and JSON time versions from our new date object.

See return image below, after we executed or ran the code. On your 'Console', all you have to do is press 'Enter'.

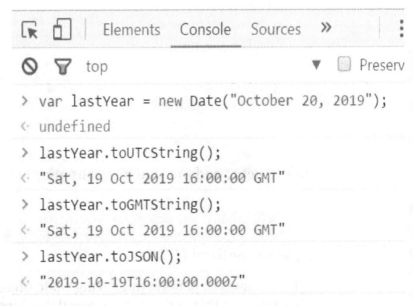

There are more complex methods of incorporating your date object into an HTML code. Again, JavaScript codes cannot exist alone, they always come with an HTML, or CSS codes.

Chapter 26: Definition and Uses of Prompts

On many websites prompts are significant tools for the users' interaction with the website. Prompts are boxes that ask users some questions and then users can either answer or not.

Prompt codes are similar to alert codes, but prompts have more interactive capabilities, such as being able to ask the user questions and allowing the user to give their own responses, or select the default response provided by the website. The alerts simply give a message or an alert to the user.

Example of prompt codes:

1   var   question   =   "Your   highest   educational attainment?";

2 var defaultAnswer = "college";

3 var educ = prompt (question, defaultAnswer);

See image below of how the prompt box appears:

```
> question = "Your highest educational
  attainment?";
< "Your highest educational attainment?"
> defaultAnswer = "college";
< "college"
> educ = prompt (question, defaultAnswer);
>
```

This page says:

Your highest educational attainment?

| college |

☐ Prevent this page from creating additional dialogs.

OK   Cancel

The user can delete the default answer, "college" and type in a new answer, or the user can click 'OK' to accept the default answer.

You may also use this JavaScript code:

```
var message = prompt('What is your name?');

    document.write(message);

var date = Date();

    document.write(date);

var location = window.location;

    document.write(location);
```

In Chrome:

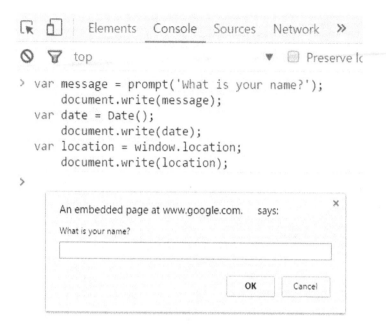

```
var message = prompt('What is your name?');
    document.write(message);
var date = Date();
    document.write(date);
var location = window.location;
    document.write(location);
```

An embedded page at www.google.com.   says:

What is your name?

OK   Cancel

In Mozilla:

Developer Tools - New Tab - about:newtab

```
var message = prompt('What is your name?');
            document.write(message);
var date = Date();
            document.write(date);
var location = window.location;
            document.write(location);
```

The date and location are added, just to show you that you can also view them on an appropriate browser.

The point is that you can easily ask questions from your website users and interact with them. This is one of the significant uses of JavaScript.

Chapter 27: Creating 'if' Condition Statements

'if' statements are used in questions that a user can respond to, and that the website has to react to when the correct answer is verified.

They always start with an 'if' word. 'if' statements, together with 'else' statements are called conditional statements because conditions are set for them to be executed.

Let's say your question is: "What is the common name of sodium chloride?"

The answer is table salt.

If the user will be able to answer correctly, you can create a prompt congratulating him.

If not, then your prompt will tell him that his answer is incorrect.

Example:

```
var x = prompt ("What is the common name of sodium
chloride?");

if (x === "table salt") {

alert ("Correct!");

}
```

See next image:

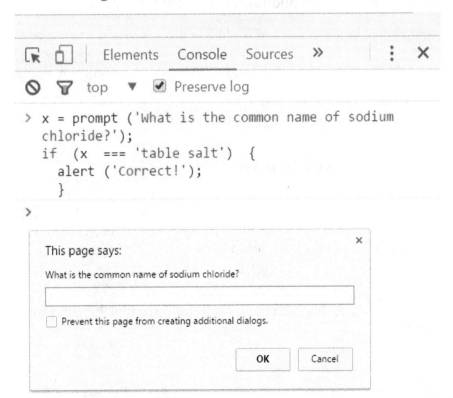

When the user is able to answer the prompt question with the correct answer, 'table salt', and press OK. The alert will pop-up with the message you have created.

See next image:

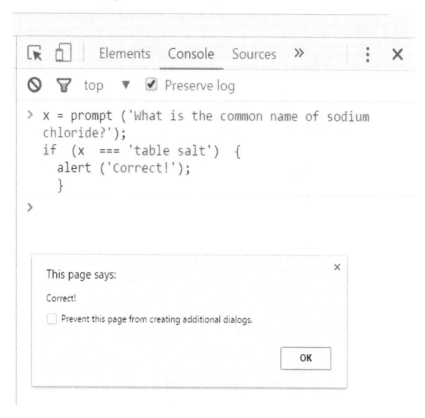

If you have noticed the image above, the word 'var' and the numbers are not reflected.

The JavaScript code has also used single quotes. This can happen.

When the code or command produces an error, you can change the type of quotes and remove unwelcome identifiers. You will still be obtaining the same results.

See next image:

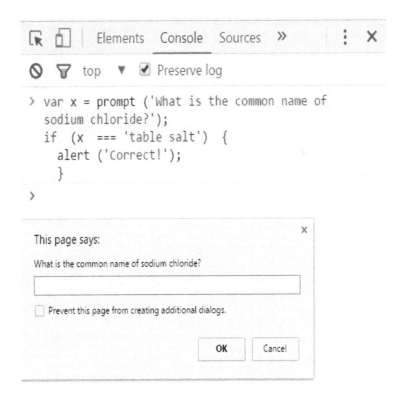

The same thing happens, when the user is able to answer correctly, the alert that you have created above will show 'Correct!'.

Let's try double quotes, if we get the same results. Based on the image below, we got the same results.

The code still worked properly.

See next image:

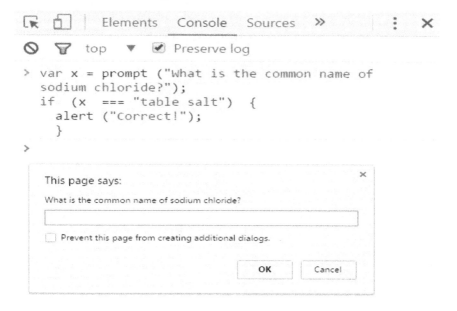

Reminders:

- The keyword for 'if' statements is the word 'if'.

- The first line of the 'if' statement ends with an opening curly bracket {

- The entire 'if' statement ends with a closing curly bracket } on the same line.

- The normal semicolon ending may not be used when there are curly brackets { } . The curly brackets are code blockers, and they indicate that the statements inside must be executed together.

- After the keyword 'if', leave a space, and then enclose your conditions in parentheses.

- The === is used instead of the = sign because the = sign is commonly used to assign values to variables. The === sign signifies equality.

- You can modify the code, as long as you attain your objective. You can do this by using a variable instead of a string.

- Two spaces can be provided before the 'alert' code. It is not required, but you can use this as one modification when you receive errors from the execution of your JavaScript codes.

Example:

var question = "What is the common name of sodium chloride?"

prompt (question);

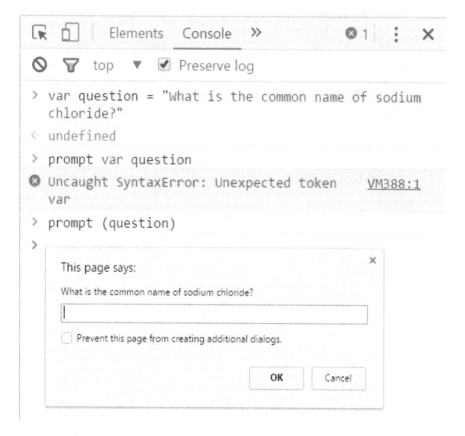

If you noticed in the above image, the semicolon was not added in the commands/statements above, but the 'Console' and browser still executed them.

In case an error occurs, like the red-lettered error in the image above, you can promptly correct the indicated error; in this case - the inclusion of 'var' in the variable's name. The name of the variable should have been 'question' only, without the word 'var'.

See image below:

- If you want several responses to the other answers of users, you can also create several statements to be executed. It's up to you. You have now the power to perform this process.

Chapter 28: Creating 'if...else' Condition Statements

'if...else' statements are the same as the 'if' statements, only, another alternative is provided by the 'else' statement.

'if...else' means that if the specified condition is not 'true' or 'possible', then the 'else' statement will be executed. It's like another option is provided by the page.

The simplest code for 'if...else' statement is this:

if (condition)

statement 1

{else

statement 2}

Example 1:

This script is used in chapter 37 in swapping images.

```
<script type = "text/javascript">
    var imageCloud =['pic1.jpg', 'pic2.jpg'];
    var pics = new Array();
```

```
for (var a in imageCloud) {
    pics[a] = new image();
    pics[a].src = imageClouds[a];
    var onPicImg1 = 0;
function swapImage (elemId) {
    switch (elemId) }

if(onPicImg1 ==0 {
onPicImg1 = 1;

} else if (onPicImg1 ==1) {
onPicImg1= 0;
}
}
</script>
```

See image below:

```
<script type = "text/javascript">
   var imageCloud =['pic1.jpg', 'pic2.jpg'];
   var pics = new Array();

for (var a in imageCloud)  {
                   pics[a] = new image();
                   pics[a].src = imageClouds[a];
           var onPicImg1 = 0;
           function swapImage (elemId)  {
           switch (elemId)  }

if(onPicImg1 ==0  {
       onPicImg1 = 1;

   } else if (onPicImg1 ==1)  {
     onPicImg1= 0;
   }
  }
 }
</script>
```

The script can get confusing at times. Keep in mind to state the 'if' and the 'else' statements properly.

Here's a simpler example: (Let's make use of the 'if' example from the previous chapter.)

Example 2:

var x = prompt ('What is the common name of sodium chloride?');

if (x === 'table salt') {

alert ('Correct!');

}

else {

alert ('Incorrect');

}

This code was executed and the prompt appeared on the page:

See image below:

Let's say the user did not give the correct answer. Let's assume she answered 'sugar'. When the user enters her answer; let's see what happens:

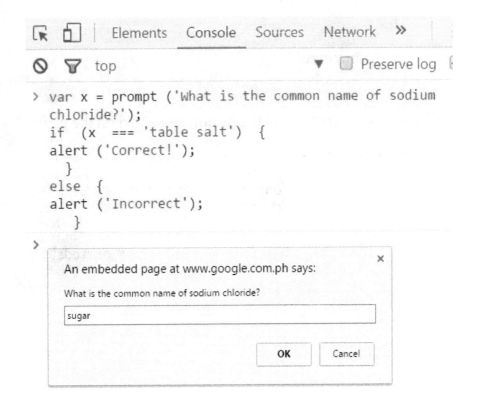

If the user clicks 'OK', another alert will appear, with the 'verdict' – "Incorrect".

See image below:

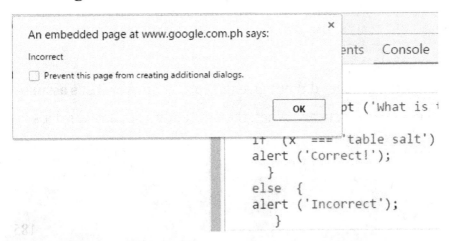

You can create more 'if…else' statements depending on the need of your web page. Go ahead and try other statements.

'if…else…if statements

These statements are used to determine if the stated conditions are true, if not, then the 'else' statement is executed.

It is the same with 'if…else', only more statements/conditions are added.

Example:

var x = prompt ("What is the common name of sodium chloride?");

if (x === "table salt") {

alert ("Correct!");

}

else if (x === "salt") {

alert ("partially correct!");

}

else {

alert ("Incorrect");

}

See next image:

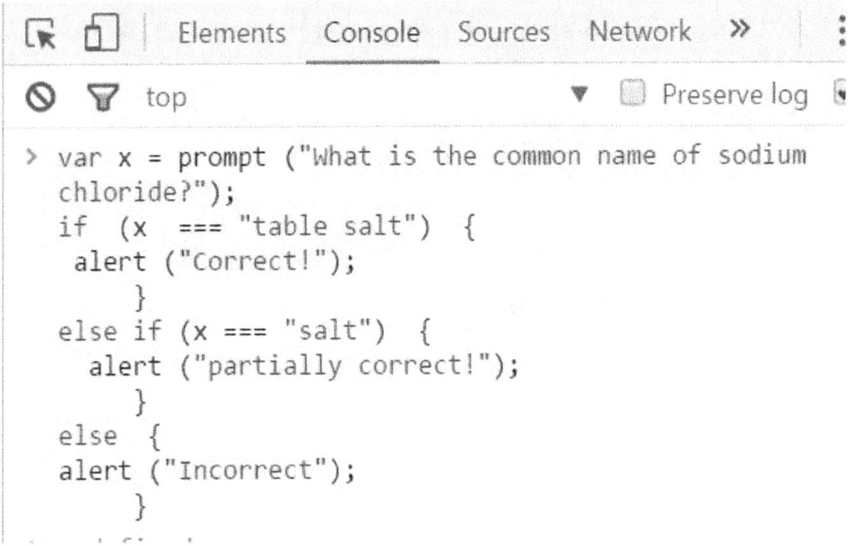

Elements
Console
Sources
Network
top
Preserve log
> var x = prompt ("What is the common name of sodium chloride?");
if (x === "table salt") {
alert ("Correct!");
}
else if (x === "salt") {
alert ("partially correct!");
}
else {
alert ("Incorrect");
}

When the user executes or enters the code above, the prompt will appear.

See image below:

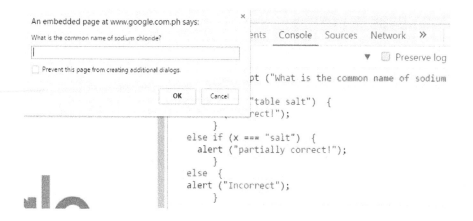

Let's assume the user has answered 'salt'.

See next image:

The 'else if' statement will then be executed, with the specified alert:

See image below:

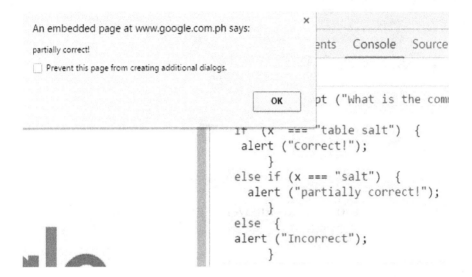

An embedded page at www.google.com.ph says:

partially correct!

☐ Prevent this page from creating additional dialogs.

OK

ents   Console   Source

pt ("What is the com

```
if (x === "table salt")  {
  alert ("Correct!");
      }
else if (x === "salt")  {
  alert ("partially correct!");
      }
else  {
  alert ("Incorrect");
      }
```

Chapter 29: Creating and Accessing Arrays

Array methods in JavaScript have significant uses that you can find essential when writing your codes. In this chapter, we will discuss the most commonly used methods. You can learn everything when you proceed with your advance lessons. Are you ready? Fire in the hole!

What is an array?

An array is useful in storing several, or multiple values in one object or variable.

Examples:

var places = ['Seoul', 'Bangkok', 'Venice', 'Cheyenne', 'New York'];

var luckyNumbers = [7, 9, 13];

var favorites = ['ice cream', 'chocolates', 'cakes', 'fruits'];

The Mozilla 'Console' recognized the entry immediately as an array and identified it as such.

See image below:

If you have created all the examples of arrays abovementioned, this is how it will appear:

If you don't use arrays, you would have to name the variables one by one, like in the example below. That would be cumbersome and time-consuming.

Examples:

var places1 = 'Seoul';

var places2 = 'Bangkok';

var places3 = 'Venice';

var places4 = 'Cheyenne';

var places5 = 'New York';

In creating your arrays, you can also use this format for your JavaScript statement: It can span multiple lines, but ascertain that you separate your values by commas, and start and end the array using brackets.

var placesToSee = [

'Seoul',

'Bangkok',

'Venice',

'Cheyenne',

'New York'

];

See image below:

```
      Developer Tools - New Tab - about:newtab        —  □  ×

  ⬚   ⬚   ⊟   ⊙   {}   ☺   ≡   ⊟▾  ⊟   ⊟   ⚙

  🗑   ●  ▾  ●  ▾  ●  ▾  ●  ▾  ●  ▾  ●  ▾   🔍 Filter o

  »  places = [
        'Seoul',
        'Bangkok',
        'Venice',
        'Cheyenne',
        'New York'
     ];
  ←  Array [ "Seoul", "Bangkok", "Venice",
     "Cheyenne", "New York" ]



  »|
```

The general syntax for creating arrays is:

var arrayName = [element1, element2, element3, ...];

The element/value may be a text or a number. The brackets are used because, usually, they indicate that the elements are being processed as a group, or simultaneously.

You can also use this statement, but there are new browsers that don't recognize it. Experiment with your browser, until you get the preferred JavaScript code:

var arrayName = new Array();

Accessing your arrays

You can access an element of the array by using this statement:

var name = arrayName[index number]

Indexes of the elements or values in an array starts with 0.

Hence, in the 'places', the 0 index is assigned to 'Seoul'; 1 for 'Bangkok'; 2 for 'Venice'; 3 for 'Cheyenne' and so on.

Example:

If you want to access 'Cheyenne', your statement would be:

var res = places[3];

See the result at the last line of the image:

```
← Array [ "Seoul", "Bangkok", "Venice",
    "Cheyenne", "New York" ]
>> luckyNumbers = [7, 9, 13];
← Array [ 7, 9, 13 ]
>> favorties = ['ice cream', 'chocolates',
    'cakes', 'fruits'];
← Array [ "ice cream", "chocolates",
    "cakes", "fruits" ]
>> res = places[3];
← "Cheyenne"
>>|
```

You can get or obtain the value of index 1 from your array (favorites) by using this statement:

Example:

> *var favorites = ['ice cream', 'chocolates', 'cakes', 'fruits'];*
>
> *var favorites[1];*

So, to access the value of any index in your array, the statement is simply:

arrayName[index];

This code will return the value "chocolates".

See image below:

If you have an array of patients namely: 'Elsa', 'Ana', 'Lily', 'Leo', you can create an array with this statement:

var patients = ['Elsa', 'Ana', 'Lily', 'Leo'];

This will return the value:

> ["Elsa", "Ana", "Lily", "Leo"]

If you're working directly on a browser, and you want to write 'Leo" on the web page, you can use this code.

Document.write(patients[3]);

This command will allow "Leo" to appear on the web page (see image down below). The white space opposite the 'Console' is the page.

You can insert the script into your HTML code too.

Therefore, you can access and write the values of the array, based on their indices. Keep in mind that indices in the computer world starts with 0, 1, 2, 3, and so on.

So, the indices of the values in your array are:

'Elsa' = 0

'Ana' = 1

'Lily' = 2

'Leo' = 3

Watch out in writing your statements because this might return an error, like the error in the image below. The closing parenthesis) sign was missing.

After the parenthesis was added, and the code was run on the browser, the result displayed the name of 'Leo" on the page.

See image below:

Leo

```
⌞▪  ⌷        Elements   Console   »      ⊗ 1  ⋮  ✕

⊘  ▽  top                          ▼  ▢ Preserve

>  patients = ['Elsa', 'Ana', 'Lily', 'Leo'];
‹  ▶ ["Elsa", "Ana", "Lily", "Leo"]
>  document.write(patients[3];
⊗ Uncaught SyntaxError: missing )        VM603:1
   after argument list
>  document.write(patients[3]);
‹  undefined
>  |
```

Reminders:

- Arrays can be used for objects.

- Arrays simplify the statement for your values.

- When you assign values for arrays in an array, these deeper arrays are also enclosed in brackets.

- In document.write, the name of the array is enclosed in parentheses, and the index is in brackets.

Knowing how to manipulate your arrays to serve your purpose is a skill that you can acquire over time.

This is because learning a computer language needs repetition and practice. You have to practice repeatedly to perfect the skill.

Chapter 30: Measuring Arrays

It's useful to know how to measure your arrays. Programmers and web developers usually measure the length property of an array. You will need this later on, when you decide to create your own interactive website.

How can you measure your arrays? Here's how to do it using the statement:

arrayName.length;

Example 1:

var patients = ["Elsa", "Ana", "Lily", "Leo];

patients.length;

The return will be = 4

Since there are 4 elements in your array.

See image below:

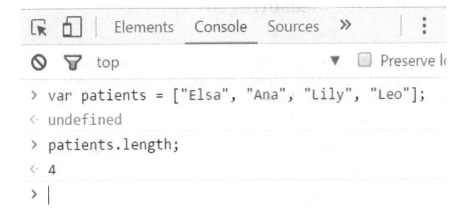

```
> var patients = ["Elsa", "Ana", "Lily", "Leo"];
< undefined
> patients.length;
< 4
> |
```

Example 2:

*var students = ["Thompson", "Lyndon", "Cruise",
"Trump", "Clinton"];*

students.length;

This will return 5.

```
⌞⌝ ⌷    Elements   Console   Security  »        ⋮  ✕

⊘  ▽  top                         ▼  ▢ Preserve log

>  var students = ["Thompson", "Lyndon", "Cruise",
   "Trump", "Clinton"];
<  undefined
>  students.length;
<  5
>
```

Reminders:

- You have to input or identify first your 'patients'
  array. This means you input first the elements of the
  'patients' into the 'Console' and press 'Enter', before
  you can measure the length.

- If you obtain an error return/report, you can
  identify what the error is all about.

- If you can't find any error, try changing your quotes;
  check if your quotes are matching each other; check
  if you have closing or opening quotes; check if you
  have the semicolon at the end of the statement;
  check if your elements are separated by commas;
  check if your arrays are enclosed in matching
  brackets. There are times, the 'Console' doesn't
  recognize the term 'var', and you have to omit it.

This is part of the learning process, the more you explore, the more you will learn. Learning entitles you to commit mistakes. But don't commit the errors over and over, that's no longer learning.

Chapter 31: Splicing Arrays

Arrays can be spliced using the keyword 'splice'. 'Splice' means removing elements from your arrays. You can remove elements you don't want and still maintain the integrity of the array.

Example:

Let's use the same array from the previous chapter.

```
var students = [

        'Thompson', 'male', 'passed',

        "Lyndon', 'female', 'passed',

        'Cruise', 'male', 'failed'
];
```

And you want to splice it.

```
students.splice(0,2);
```

Where:

0 – is the index you want to start from

2 – is the number of elements you want to remove

Hence, in the code, *students.splice(0,2);* you want to start from "Thompson" and remove 2 elements.

See image below:

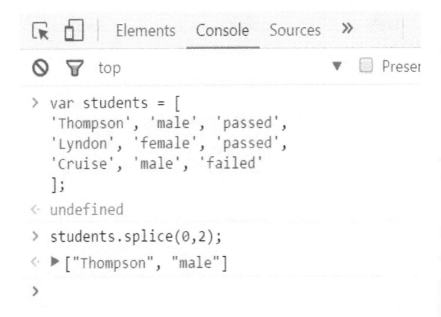

Again, the indices are assigned this way, for the first index:

"Thompson" = 1

"Lyndon" = 2

"Cruise" = 3

The indices for the second index are these:

Name = 0

Gender = 1

Grade = 2

Therefore, the code, students.splice(0,2) showed ["Thompson", "male"].

Chapter 32: Looping Arrays

You can loop though arrays too. Looping is repeating the array as many times as you want.

Loops are useful in maintaining records and repeated data files.

'for' loops

Example:

```
var students = ["Landon", "Putin", "Trump", "Clinton", "Walker"];
for (var x = 0; x < name.length;  x++) {
    console.log(name[x]);
}
```

See image below:

```
Developer Tools - New Tab - about:newtab          - ☐
```

```
>>    students = ['Landon', 'Putin', 'Trump',
      'Clinton', 'Walker'];
←    Array [ "Landon", "Putin", "Trump",
      "Clinton", "Walker" ]
```

Elements   Console   Sources   »   ⋮   ✕

🚫 🔽 top   ▼ ☐ Preserve log

```
> var students = ['Landon', 'Putin', 'Trump',
  'Clinton', 'Walker'];
< undefined
> for (var x = 0; x < name.length;  x++) {
      console.log(name[x]);
      }
< undefined
> for (var x = 0; x < students.length;  x++) {
      console.log(students[x]);
  }
  Landon                                 VM83:2
  Putin                                  VM83:2
  Trump                                  VM83:2
  Clinton                                VM83:2
  Walker                                 VM83:2
< undefined
```

'while' loops

Example:

```
var t = 0;

while (t < 10) {
    console.log("Iteration: " + t);
        t++;
}
```

When this command or code is executed or entered, the result will be this:

```
> var t = 0;

  while (t < 10)  {
            console.log('Iteration: '  + t);
        t++;
  }

  Iteration: 0

  Iteration: 1

  Iteration: 2

  Iteration: 3

  Iteration: 4

  Iteration: 5

  Iteration: 6

  Iteration: 7

  Iteration: 8

  Iteration: 9
< 9
```

The iteration (repetition) specified is less than 10, so the return values gave up to 9 Iterations. If you change the JavaScript code to:

var t = 0;

```
while (t < 15) {
    console.log('Iteration: ' + t);
    t++;
}
```

The return values would be this:

Iteration: 0

Iteration: 1

Iteration: 2

Iteration: 3

Iteration: 4

Iteration: 5

Iteration: 6

Iteration: 7

Iteration: 8

Iteration: 9

Iteration: 10

Iteration: 11

Iteration: 12

Iteration: 13

Iteration: 14

14

'do - while' loop

You can do this type of loop through the following statements:

Example:

```
var t = 0;

do {

    console.log("Iteration: " + t);

        t++;

}

while (t< 10);
```

When this code is executed, the result is this:

See image below

```javascript
> var t = 0;
        do {
      console.log("Iteration: " + t);
          t++;
        }
      while (t< 10);
  Iteration: 0
  Iteration: 1
  Iteration: 2
  Iteration: 3
  Iteration: 4
  Iteration: 5
  Iteration: 6
  Iteration: 7
  Iteration: 8
  Iteration: 9
< 9
```

Based on the examples above, you can iterate or repeat a specified element in an array, several times as you wish. Just take note of the correct code.

You can change the name of the array according to your preferences, as long as you make sure that the name you used throughout the code is correct and consistent. Letter 't' was just my preference.

Chapter 33: Multi and Two-Dimensional Arrays

Multi or two-dimensional arrays indicate that there will be two or more indices involved because there will be many or two arrays that would be utilized. In summary, there will be arrays in arrays, or an array in an array.

We'll use our first example in the simple array to demonstrate the two-dimensional or multi-dimensional array. We have previously used the single quotes but let's start using double quotes this time, to show you that both work in your JavaScript codes.

If our simple array is:

var patients = ["Elsa", "Ana", "Lily", "Leo"];

Now, let's create an array of two or more of values in your simple arrays. We can write the structure of our statement this way to facilitate the creation of the multi, or two dimensional arrays.

You should write your statement properly, so you can easily create arrays within the array.

Example:

var patients = [

"Elsa",

"Ana",

"Lily",

"Leo'

];

You can then create arrays out of each of the values/elements from your simple array.

See example below:

var patients = [

    ["Elsa", "married", 30, "Chicago", "idiopathic anemia"],

    ["Ana", "single", 18, "Laramie", "viral hepatitis"],

    ["Lily", "married", 38, "San Diego", "diabetes mellitus"],

    ["Leo", "married", 45, "San Francisco", "essential hypertension"]

    ];

You have created multi-dimensional arrays from your simple array, by adding more relevant information about the patients.

This is essential when you have various users' data in your website and you want to store them, so you can access them anytime.

Accessing multi or two-dimensional arrays

You can do this with this statement:

document.write(patients [] []);

The two matching brackets indicate the indexes of two arrays. The first bracket indicates the index of the value or element you need from the main array, and the second bracket indicates the index of the value in your second array that you would like to print.

Don't forget the default rule that all indices start at 0, 1, 2, 3, and so on.

Example from our previous array:

var patients = [

['Elsa', 'married', 30, 'Chicago', 'idiopathic anemia'],

['Ana', 'single', 18, 'Laramie', 'viral hepatitis'],

['Lily', 'married', 38, 'San Diego', 'diabetes mellitus'],

['Leo', 'married', 45, 'San Francisco', 'essential hypertension']

    ];

See image below: (from Mozilla)

Let's say you want to access, display or print "Elsa's" data, specifically her illness, "idiopathic anemia".

You can write your JavaScript this way:

document.write(patients([0] [4]);

Where:

[0] – indicates the first index in your patients' array, and that index is 'Elsa', and the second bracket [4], indicates index 4, which is Elsa's illness – 'idiopathic anemia'.

This statement (document.write(patients[0] [4]); will write "idiopathic anemia" on your web page.

See image below: (from Chrome)

idiopathic
anemia

```
  Elements   Console  »

  top  ▼   Preserve log

> patients = [
        ['Elsa', 'married', 30, 'Chicago',
   'idiopathic anemia'],
        ['Ana', 'single', 18, 'Laramie',
   'viral hepatitis'],
        ['Lily', 'married', 38, 'San Diego',
   'diabetes mellitus'],
        ['Leo', 'married', 45, 'San
   Francisco', 'essential hypertension']
   ];
  ▶ [Array[5], Array[5], Array[5], Array[5]]
> document.write(patients[0][4]);
```

Hence the indices of your arrays are:

For the first bracket:

'Elsa' = 0

'Ana' = 1

'Lily' = 2

'Leo' = 3

For the second bracket:

Name = 0

Civil status = 1

Age = 2

State = 3

Illness = 4

If you can follow so far, we can now proceed to having a third bracket. You can stand up and stretch your muscles for a while. You're not running a race. Easy, does it. Learn at your own pace. That's one advantage of using a book.

You may go over the lessons above one more time, or several times, until you can understand fully.

Nonetheless, here's how you add the third bracket. These are called 'nested' arrays. You can go as deep as you wish.

The third bracket can come from an array in the array of the original array; quite confusing, you might say.

Yes, it is. It's easier to think of nested items, to visualize the arrays.

Let's use the second example above:

You can insert another bracket inside the bracket of the patients' data, to create a third nested array. Let's say you have decided to include the severity ('mild') of the illness, and the treatment for it ('iron').

var patients = [

[‘Elsa’, ‘married’, 30, ‘Chicago’, ‘idiopathic anemia’, [‘mild’, ‘iron’]],

[‘Ana’, ‘single’, 18, ‘Laramie’, ‘viral hepatitis’, [‘severe’, ‘antiviral’]],

[‘Lily’, ‘married’, 38, ‘San Diego’, ‘diabetes mellitus’],

[‘Leo’, ‘married’, 45, ‘San Francisco’, ‘essential hypertension’]

];

See image below:

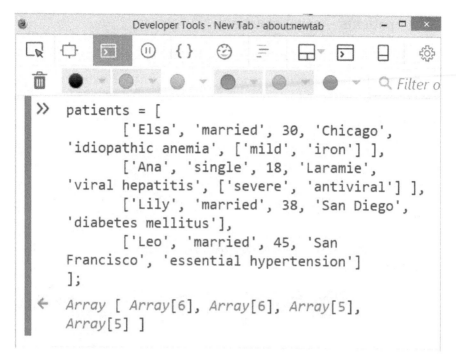

```
>>  patients = [
        ['Elsa', 'married', 30, 'Chicago',
    'idiopathic anemia', ['mild', 'iron'] ],
        ['Ana', 'single', 18, 'Laramie',
    'viral hepatitis', ['severe', 'antiviral'] ],
        ['Lily', 'married', 38, 'San Diego',
    'diabetes mellitus'],
        ['Leo', 'married', 45, 'San
    Francisco', 'essential hypertension']
    ];
←   Array [ Array[6], Array[6], Array[5],
    Array[5] ]
```

In Elsa's data, we have added brackets to describe the severity of her illness ('mild'), and the kind of treatment that she had ('iron').

You may or may not add these information to the rest of the arrays, it's up to you.

When you want to access Elsa's data on her illness, and how severe it is, you can use this statement:

document.write(patients[0][5][0]);

Where:

patients – name of array

[0] – index number of Elsa. Read explanations below:

Indices

0   ['Elsa', 'married', 30, 'Chicago', 'idiopathic anemia' ['mild', 'iron']],

1   ['Ana', 'single', 18, 'Laramie', 'viral hepatitis', ['severe', 'antiviral']],

2   ['Lily', 'married', 38, 'San Diego', 'diabetes mellitus'],

3   ['Leo', 'married', 45, 'San Francisco', 'essential hypertension']

Or, use the original array:

var patients = ['Elsa', 'Ana', 'Lily', 'Leo']

Indices   0   1   2   3

[5] – index number of the array describing her illness

['Elsa', 'married', 30, 'Chicago', 'idiopathic anemia' ['mild', 'iron']],

Indices - 0   1   2   3   4   5

[0] – index number of the elements of the fifth array.

['mild', 'iron']

Indices -   0   1

The indices of the third bracket are:

Severity of the illness = 0 ('mild')

Kind of treatment = 1 ('iron')

Therefore, the index inside the third bracket is 0, because you want to access the severity of the illness.

The return value of your code: document.write(patients[0][5][0]); would be - "mild".

See image below:

mild

```
> patients = [
        ["Elsa", "married", 30, "Chicago",
   "idiopathic anemia", ["mild", "iron"] ],
        ["Ana", "single", 18, "Laramie",
   "viral hepatitis", ["severe", "antiviral"]
   ],
        ["Lily", "married", 38, "San Diego",
   "diabetes mellitus"],
        ["Leo", "married", 45, "San
   Francisco", "essential hypertension"]
   ];
< ▶ [Array[6], Array[6], Array[5], Array[5]]
> document.write(patients[0][5][0]);
< undefined
>
```

You can add or insert as many arrays as you want. Simply follow the method in accessing them, so you can obtain the correct data. The key is to bear in mind that indices always start with 0.

A toast for you for having gone this far. Experts would breeze through this chapter, but for you as a beginner, I know you will consider it a victory to learn about multi-dimensional arrays. Bravo!

Chapter 34: Changing Elements in Multi-Dimensional Arrays

Although, this is one complicated process for you, you can still learn the basics here.

When changing the elements in an array, the procedure is similar to accessing your arrays - only – you will have to specify what elements you need to change and what changes you want to implement.

Let's use our previous array, on patients, for this chapter, so you can understand more.

Example:

var patients = [

['Elsa', 'married', 30, 'Chicago', 'idiopathic anemia', ['mild', 'iron']],

['Ana', 'single', 18, 'Laramie', 'viral hepatitis', ['severe', 'antiviral']],

['Lily', 'married', 38, 'San Diego', 'diabetes mellitus'],

['Leo', 'married', 45, 'San Francisco', 'essential hypertension']

];

If you want to change the treatment for the disease of "Elsa", from "iron" to "proper nutrition", you can use this code:

patients[0][5][1]= 'proper nutrition';

Where:

    patients = name of array

    [0] – index of 'Elsa'

    [5] – index of severity and treatment

    [1] – index of treatment

    'proper nutrition' – text to change 'iron'

When you access the information using this code:

document.write(patients[0][5][1]);

The return value will be:

    'proper nutrition'

Quite easy, huh! More practice and you'll learn it by heart.

Identifying the index was explained in the previous chapter.

Chapter 35: Document Object Model

DOM or Document Object Model is used by all web pages. HTML and XML has this programming interface. This model is like a lineage tree that starts from parents and then branches out to children, grandchildren, and great, great grandchildren.

This 'tree' has nodes, and each node can branch or go deeper depending on how the web language programmer structured it.

A web page has documents, elements that have attributes you can change with JavaScript.

Why are we discussing it here? Because JavaScript is a powerful language that can modify, enhance and help structure the web page to become more interactive, user-friendly and appealing to users with the help of the DOM.

JavaScript can find an element in the content of a web page and interact with it using the DOM, through the API (Application Programming Interface). Take note that the API of all browsers is the same.

Obviously, JavaScript may not be the only programming language that can do these actions, but certainly, JavaScript is the most common choice and the favorite language of web developers.

Accessing the DOM

You can access the DOM through the API. Since all browsers have the same DOM, this won't be a problem for you.

DOM methods

These are actions that you can do to the HTML elements. Elements are contained in paragraphs.

Example:

document.getElementbyId(id)

As soon as you start typing document.get... the rest of the option will appear on a drop-down menu, and you can select from there.

Don't forget to add the parentheses at the end though, specifying what element you want to interact with or modify, and the semicolon, indicating that it's the end of the statement.

See image below:

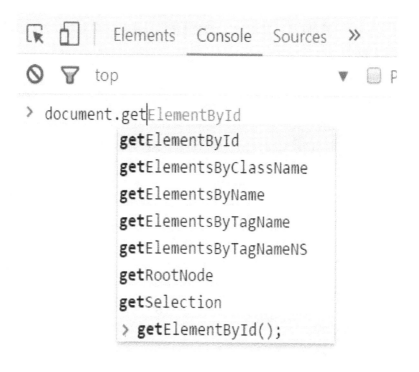

Other methods are:

Element.removeAttribute(attribute);

element.setAttribute(attribute, value);

element.innerHTML;

element.style;

DOM properties

These are values of the HTML elements that you can change or set. Each of these elements has attributes that JavaScript can interact with.

Chapter 36: Inserting JavaScript Codes into HTML

You have read earlier in the lessons that JavaScript cannot stand alone to build a web page. You have to insert the JavaScript into the <head> or <body> of the HTML code, or link externally the JavaScript to the page.

Having that crucial information, now, it's time you get some basic knowledge on inserting your scripts.

For what purpose did you try hard to learn JavaScript codes, if you can't actually insert them into an HTML?

Understandably, information about HTML codes is important for you to be able to do that, but HTML codes is altogether another type of programming language that deserves an entire book, as well.

I can't do that all at the same time because HTML alone can span hours and hours of discussions.

So, I'll be presenting the most basic HTML code for a page, simply for the purpose of showing you where and how to insert your JavaScript codes.

1. In HTML, there are opening and closing tags.

Whenever you open an element, value or data, there are tags that you open and close.

Opening tags are enclosed in arrows, or the greater than and lesser than symbols <>.

Closing tags use a slash, together with the arrows, to indicate it's the closing tag </>

Example:

<script>

</script>

2. The basic HTML code is this:

<html>

<head>

</head>

<body>

</body>

</html>

See image below:

233

```
File  Edit  Format  View  Help
<html>
<head>
</head>
<body>
</body>
</html>
```

Since you can insert your JavaScript into the body, or the head of the HTML, you can do it this way:

Where to insert your JavaScript code:

<html>

<head>

<script>

insert JavaScript here

</script>

</head>

<body>

</body>

</html>

See image below:

```
File   Edit   Format   View   Help
<html>
<head>
        <script>
           insert JavaScript here
        </script>
</head>
<body>
</body>
</html>
```

Or this way:

<html>

<head>

</head>

<body>

<script>

insert JavaScript here

</script>

</body>

</html>

See image below:

```
File   Edit   Format   View   Help
<html>
<head>
</head>
<body>
        <script>
         insert JavaScript here
        </script>
</body>
</html>
```

Notice that all of the elements of the HTML code have opening and closing tags.

3. Inserting a 'Prompt'.

If you have decided to insert a 'Prompt', all you have to do is to insert the code where the tags 'script' are:

See example below:

```
<html>
<head>
    <script>
        var welcome = prompt("What is your name?");
        document.write(welcome);
        console.log(welcome);
    </script>
</head>
<body>
</body>
</html>
```

See image below:

```
File  Edit  Format  View  Help
<html>
<head>
        <script>
        var welcome = prompt("What is your name?");
        document.write(welcome);
        console.log(welcome);
        </script>

</head>
<body>
</body>
</html>
```

4. **You may also want to use this method:**

<html>

<head>

</head>

<body>

   <p id="demo"></p>

   <script>

   document.getElementbyId("demo").innerHTML ="Hello World!";

   </script>

</body>

</html>

See image below:

```
File  Edit  Format  View  Help
<html>
<head>
</head>
<body>
        <p id="demo"></p>
        <script>
        document.getElementbyId("demo").innerHTML="Hello World!";
        </script>
</body>
</html>
```

Insert any type of JavaScript codes into the <script> </script> tags, and you'll be okay.

There you go. Do you know now, where and how to insert your Javascript codes? You can practice more, if you're up to it.

Chapter 37: Manipulating and Swapping Images

In maintaining the good appearance of your website, you may need to manipulate and swap images. You can do this through the following methods:

Using the getElementById();

You can change or swap images by using a JavaScript code inserted/embedded into the HTML code.

Example:

```
<!DOCTYPE html>
<html>
<head>
    <meta charset="utf-8"/>
    <script type="text/javascript">
    Function change() {
    var image =
document.getElementById('landscape');
    }
    </script>
</head>
<body>
```

<img src= "//indicate the source of the image";>

</body>

</html>

See next image:

```
File  Edit  Format  View  Help
<!DOCTYPE html>
<html>
<head>
        <meta charset="utf-8"/>
          <script type="text/javascript">
            Function change() {
            var image = document.getElementById('landscape');
              }
            </script>
</head>
<body>
  <img src= "//indicate the source of the image";>
</body>
</html>
```

Take note of the slight difference with the previous HTML codes that we have used. You can see the:

<!DOCTYPE html> and *<script type="text/javascript">*.

This is the same as the opening of the script tag, which is <script>

The // indicates that the text is a comment and is not part of the HTML script.

Remember to add the closing tag of your JavaScript, </script>. The HTML script here is merely the basic codes, so you will see where the JavaScript code can be inserted.

In this case, when a user clicks on the image, it will change.

Another example of JavaScript to be inserted is this:

<script type="text/javascript">

Function changeImage(image ID, imageFileName)

{

var image= document.getElementById(Image ID).src = imageFileName;

}

</script>

See image below:

```
File  Edit  Format  View  Help
    <script type="text/javascript">
    Function changeImage(image ID, imageFileName)
    {
    var image= document.getElementById(Image ID).src = imageFileName;
    }
    </script>
```

Using 'if - else' statement

You can swap images back and forth by using JavaScript's 'if' statement.

However, these images must be of the same sizes, and they should be stored together with your data. In addition, they must be preloaded.

```
!DOCTYPE html>

<html>

<head>

    <meta charset="utf-8"/>

        <script type = "text/javascript">
        var imageCloud =['pic1.jpg', 'pic2.jpg'];
        var pics = new Array();

        for (var a in imageCloud) {
        pics[a] = new image();
        pics[a].src = imageCloud[a];
        var onPicImg1 = 0;
        function swapImage (elemId) {
         switch (elemId) }

        if(onPicImg1 ==0 {
        onPicImg1 = 1;
        }
        else if (onPicImg1 ==1) {
        onPicImg1= 0;
            }
        }
        </script>

</head>

<body>
```

```
<div>
<img src= "//indicate the source of the image";>
</div>
</body>
</html>
```

See next image:

```
<!DOCTYPE html>
<html>
<head>
        <meta charset="utf-8"/>
                <script type = "text/javascript">
                var imageCloud =['pic1.jpg', 'pic2.jpg'];
                var pics = new Array();

                for (var a in imageCloud)  {
                        pics[a] = new image();
                pics[a].src = imageCloud[a];
                var onPicImg1 = 0;
                function swapImage (elemId)  {
                 switch (elemId)  }

                if(onPicImg1 ==0  {
                onPicImg1 = 1;
                }
                else if (onPicImg1 ==1)  {
                onPicImg1= 0;
                        }
                 }
                </script>
</head>
<body>
<div>
 <img src= "//indicate the source of the image";>
</div>
</body>
</html>
```

There are still other methods to manipulate and swap your images, and I'm sure you will learn more as you proceed to your advance lessons.

These codes may not be perfect, so you can experiment and modify them, and find out what works with your browser. Learning entails freedom to learn through your mistakes.

What's important is that you know the basic HTML code, which is:

<!DOCTYPE html>

<html>

<head>

</head>

<body>

</body>

</html>

See image below:

```
File  Edit  Format  View  Help
<!DOCTYPE html>
<html>
<head>
</head>
<body>
</body>
</html>
```

And your JavaScript code for HTML, which is:

```
<script type = "text/javascript">
//insert JavaScript code here
</script>
```

Or simply:

```
<script>
//insert JavaScript code here
</script>
```

Again, you can insert the whole JavaScript code into the <head> or <body> parts of your HTML.

Have fun tweaking your JavaScript and HTML codes and discover a new amazing world of computer languages.

Chapter 38: Controlling Windows Using JavaScript

Yes, JavaScript can also control your Windows size and fill it. By now, you're familiar with how powerful JavaScript is in developing your webpage and making it interactive.

Now, let's skim a bit on how JavaScript can control your windows.

Opening a new window

You can open a new window with JavaScript by using the code:

window.open("foo.html", "windowName");

From this JavaScript statement, you can do various things, such as resizing it, moving it, or adding or removing the menu bars, or title bars.

You can add additional codes to let this happen. Let's say you want to call your new window – amazingWorld, this is how you can write the JavaScript statements.

window.open("foo.html", "amazingWorld",

"width =350, height=350, scrollbars=yes, titlebars=no");

Resizing windows

To resize your window, you can use the keywords: 'resizeTo' and 'resize By'. You can try testing your browser by using the code below:

window.resizeBy(100,-100);

You may want to resize your window not less than 100 pixels, because some browsers will not allow this action.

Closing your windows

To close your window, you can use the code:

nameOfWindow.close();

In this case, your JavaScript code would be:

amazingWorld.close();

There are still more complex codes in accessing global frames and global variables of other pages, but you can learn all of these in your JavaScript advance lessons. If we take them up now, you may forget the basic codes and get confused in the process.

Take note:

- The height, width, top (position), left (position) elements are expressed in numbers.

- The different window bars (toolbars, scrollbars, menubars, titlebars), location, status and resizable elements are expressed in Boolean (yes or no).

- Many browsers won't allow you to create a window with a width and length that is less than 100 pixels. However, don't fill the whole screen with your window, it's not user friendly.

- It's not advisable to move and position of your window, if you don't have to. Allow your browser to place it where it can be moved.

Chapter 39: Accessing Style Sheets Using JavaScript

You may have to create new style sheets for your website later on, when you become a web developer and programmer.

JavaScript can access style sheets from the browser for you.

CSS or Cascading Style Sheets are responsible in displaying HTML elements on a website using markup language. HTML and CSS are crucial in building websites.

Accessing style sheets

JavaScript can access style sheets by using this code:

document.styleSheets

You can also use the code:

document.createElement

If you want to create new style sheets, use this code:

var sheet = document.createElement('style')

sheet.innerHTML = "div{border: 3px navy blue; background color: yellow;}";

document.body.appendChild(sheet);

See next image:

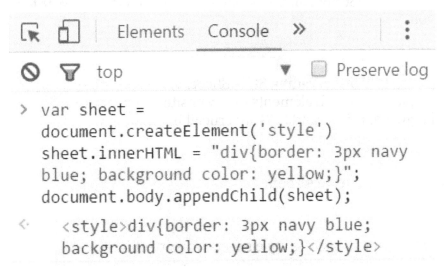

Removing style sheets

You may have to remove style sheets for some vital reason. If you want to, you can remove the style sheet promptly with this code:

var sheetRemove = document.getElementById('styleSheetId');

var sheetParent = sheetRemove.parentNode;

```
sheetParent.removeChild(sheetRemove);
```

Changing elements style

You can also change the elements style by using this code:

```
document.styleSheets[0].addRule(elements);

document.styleSheets[0].insertRule(elements);
```

or change them individually:

```
var title=document.getElementById("page-title");

title.setAttribute("style", "left: 30px");

title.style.color = "red";

title.style.backgroundColor ="green";
```

CSS is a different language on its own, so you may want to learn about it in another book.

What's important is that now you know how you can modify, add and remove style sheets using your JavaScript.

Chapter 40: Testing Popup Blockers

Through JavaScript, you can test for popup blockers. You can create an 'if – else' statement, and insert it in the <head> portion of your HTML code. See example below:

```
<DOCTYPE html>

<html>

<head>

<script>

function checkPopup() {

  var windowName = 'jsBeginner';

  var winCheck = window.open('/popup-page.php,
jsBeginner',height=350,width=540,left=24, top=24,
menubar=no, resizable=no,scrollbars=no');

  if (!winCheck) {

      alert("Please disable the popup blocker and click
"Open" again.");

      } else {

  winCheck.close();

          alert("Thanks for the visit. Popup blocker is not
detected.");

      }

  }

  window.onload = checkPopup;
```

```
</script>

</head>

<body>

</body>

</html>
```

See image below:

```
File  Edit  Format  View  Help

DOCTYPE html>
<html>
<head>

<script>
 function checkPopup() {
   var windowName = 'jsBeginner';
 var winCheck = window.open('/popup-page.php, jsBeginner',
 height=350,width=540,left=24, top=24,
menubar=no, resizable=no,scrollbars=no');
   if (!winCheck) {
     alert("Please disable the popup blocker and click "Open" again.");
     } else {
     winCheck.close();
        alert("Thanks for the visit. Popup blocker is not detected.");
   }
 }
window.onload = checkPopup;
</script>

</head>
<body>
</body>
```

There are other codes that you can create to insert your popup blocker checker. As I repeatedly mentioned through all the chapters, the JavaScript codes may not work on your browser, so you have to investigate and learn why.

255

The error prompts will indicate what went wrong, you can follow the instructions from there and correct your code.

Sometimes, the errors are caused by trivial things, such as omitted quotes; or conversion of double quotes to single quotes; matching quote was wrong (instead of using both double quotes, the opening quote is single, and the closing quote is double); a missing parenthesis, and similar occurrences.

Chapter 41: Handling JavaScript Errors and Exceptions

JavaScript errors are inevitable. It's good to face them head-on, and know what they are all about.

Committing an error means you're practicing in writing your codes. Therefore, it also indicates you're learning more.

Having said that, not all errors though, are caused by scripters or programmers, like you.

There are also errors caused by different factors, other than the scripter, himself. This could be a slight deviation from the coding set of rules, and similar incidents.

Although, there are prompters in the 'Console' that would help you resolve the issue, it's best that you become familiar with the common errors.

Common JavaScript errors

In general, there are three types of JavaScript errors:

1. **Syntax (parsing) errors**

Syntax errors deal with the JavaScript code itself. Thus, check and parse your code for any missing operators or signs.

2. Logical errors

These errors occur when your 'logic' in creating your JavaScript programs are not logical, resulting to errors. When this occurs, you have to perform a careful evaluation and analysis of the program or code you have prepared.

3. Runtime (exception) errors

These errors occur when your code is correct and has been executed, but the method you're calling no longer exists. Only the thread that has the error is affected and not the other parts.

Resolving errors

1. Throw method

You can throw your errors to the try..catch block and allow these two blocks to resolve the issue. The benefit of throwing your errors is that you can test them. This makes debugging easier and quicker.

The basic JavaScript code for this is:

throw new Error("message");

Examples:

throw new Date();

throw 3457;

When you throw an error, your try..catch block must be able to catch it, to be able to handle the error.

2. Try..catch method

This method uses the 'try' first, and then the 'catch' method in handling the errors. The basic code for this is:

```
try {
    function()
} catch(e) {
    alert(e)
}
```

Where e – exception object or errors.

A more detailed code is this:

```
try
{
    try statements;
}
```

```
catch(exception)

{

catch statements;

}
```

3. Try..catch..finally method

```
try {

try statements;

} catch(exception e) {

catch statements;

} finally {

    finally statements;

}
```

When an exception in the code appears, the 'try..block' will pass it on to the 'catch' block, so it can be remedied.

However, the 'try..catch..finally block cannot catch syntax errors. If the error is not a syntax error, the 'try block will pass the error to the 'catch block', and then, to the 'finally block'.

In the try block, the statements, after the exception occurred, will not be executed. Therefore, when an error happens in the 'try' block, subsequent statements in the block won't be executed.

Whether there's an exception or not, the 'finally block' will execute its code. It cleans the script of any 'holders' during the execution of the code.

If there are no exceptions only the 'try' and 'finally' block statements will be executed but not the 'catch' block statements.

During the creation of your codes, you'll notice that there are notices or prompters telling you what's wrong with your JavaScript codes. You'll have to follow the instructions of these error warnings, and everything will turn out well.

Chapter 42: Important Tips for JavaScript Coders

To help you in enjoying your new role as a JavaScript coder, here is a summary of significant tips that you have to follow:

1. Believe in yourself

You cannot do any simple task without believing in yourself. If you're familiar with the quotation: "Faith can move mountains', then this is time to apply it. The mind is a powerful tool in developing your skills. Try psyching yourself every day that you can do it, and you can.

2. Learn at your own pace.

Learning is not a race, so learn at your own pace. You can read a chapter or two, and understand them before proceeding. If you feel sleepy in the process, then, by all means, take a nap. That's the advantage of learning from a book.

3. Make learning fun.

Learning is fun. Throw away the notion that you have to crease your eyebrows and frown, when learning difficult stuff. Smile as you read along the chapters, and welcome the texts warmly. You can listen to soft music, while writing your codes. You can play with the statements, and observe what happens in the return values, when you execute them, or press 'Enter'.

4. Don't be afraid to fail.

Failure is a part of winning. How can you appreciate your triumph, when you haven't tasted defeat? Be thankful for your failures because they act as stepping stones to your success.

5. Review the chapters every now and then.

You can always review the chapters whenever you have forgotten any information. You should not memorize, but instead, you should understand the information, so you won't have to memorize them.

6. Be willing to explore.

Explore other languages and apps, such as Python, HTML, CSS and JAVA, because all of these are interrelated. Certainly, your knowledge would be enriched more.

7. There are several ways to skin a cat.

If you find out that there are other ways to write a code for a certain program, be ready to learn from it. JavaScript is a dynamic language and as developments in technology continue, it's expected that JavaScript would also evolve with the times.

8. Adjust to your browser's capabilities.

Your browser will help you write your statements, so befriend it. Know its capabilities and limitations and work around them. For JavaScript coding, I recommend Google Chrome and Mozilla.

9. Brackets are for arrays.

This is one important fact that you should remember. If you don't use the brackets for your arrays, they won't be recognized as such. The code may become valid initially but your succeeding statements won't hold water.

10. Quotes are for strings.

Quotes can be used for elements inside arrays and other uses. But the one thing that indicates a text or a group of text is a string is through the quotes before and after the words.

11. Semicolons are for statements.

If you're done writing your statements, ALWAYS add the semicolon. If you're writing arrays, double check if you have added the semicolon after your statements. It may be optional for some browsers, but it pays to be cautious.

12. JavaScript is different from JAVA.

JAVA has nothing to do with JavaScript. They're different things.

13. Learn more about HTML.

Continue learning about JavaScript and proceed to HTML, if you still haven't studied it. This is because HTML is the eternal host of JavaScript. Their strong and inevitable relationship will, surely, span a long time. Thus, learn about HTML, as well.

14. Continue acquiring knowledge.

Computer language is broad, and learning never stops. Develop a habit of reading new information about JavaScript.

15. JavaScript EVENTS are crucial in a web page's interactivity.

But the events involve not only involves JavaScript but CSS and HTML MARKUP languages, as well. Therefore, events complex and are recommended for advance lessons. The events include user's activity on the website, his mouse clicks, his interaction with your prompts, his mouse over, and similar events.

16. Start your own web page.

Now, take the bold move of creating your own JavaScript on your web pages. Start your own website, and enjoy the perks of knowing how to create JavaScript codes.

There you go! Now, you have ample information as a JavaScript beginner. It's time for you to spread your wings, and fly into the amazing world of JavaScript. Fly high!

Chapter 43: Quiz on JavaScript Basics

To evaluate whether you have learned something from this book, let's have a short quiz.

Remember that if you fail the quiz, it doesn't mean you're a failure. It's just that you have to review again the contents of this book. It takes REPITITION and PRACTICE to learn a new language.

You haven't failed yet, unless you stop trying. Sharpen your pencils - so to speak - and grab a paper, or use your laptop.

Quiz

Instructions: Answer first all the questions before checking the correct answers.

Write the JavaScript codes of the following:

1. Alert on your web page that would greet your visitors.

2. Prompt that states: "How are you today?"

3. An array of tourist places in the U.S.

4. A multi-dimensional array of your answer to no. 3.

5. Obtaining and displaying the value of index 3 in your answer to no. 3.

6. Displaying the date and time during the moment you're answering this quiz.

7. A variable named 'employees', and define the variable.

8. Changing the index 2 of your answer to no. 3 to "Yellowstone National Park".

9. Solving the 10^{15} expression using the JavaScript 'Console'.

10. Printing or displaying the result of your answer to no. 8.

Matching Type

Match column B with column A

Column A
Column B

1. Containers for data   A.
   program/code

2. True or false data   B. (=)

3. Symbols that enclose strings   C.
   brackets

4. Symbols that enclose arrays   D.
   comma

5. Symbol for equal value   E. var

6. Symbol to assign values   F.
   statements

7. Indicates that the statement is   G.
   variables

   done   H.
   semicolon

8. Separates values from one another

    I. (==)

9. The keyword for variable parentheses

    J.

10. A group of JavaScript statements Boolean

    K.

    L. VAR

    M. strings

    N. <=>

Chapter 44: Answers to JavaScript Quiz

Here are the answers to the JavaScript quiz:

Instructions: Write the JavaScript codes of the following:

1. Alert on your web page that would greet your visitors.

   alert("Hello, welcome to my website!");

   This JavaScript code is then inserted between <script> and </script>, in the <head> or <body> of the HTML of your page.

   <html>

   <head>

      <script>

      alert("Hello, welcome to my website!");

      </script>

   </head>

   <body>

   </body>

   </html>

   See image below:

```
 File   Edit   Format   View   Help
<html>
<head>

    <script>
    alert("Hello, welcome to my website!");
    </script>

</head>
<body>
</body>
</html>
```

This only an example. Obviously, you can create your own text greetings. It doesn't matter what words you would want to alert your visitors to.

But ensure that your function word is in the lowercase 'alert'; your string is inside matching quotes; and the whole string is enclosed in open and close parentheses.

2. Prompt that states: "How are you today?"

   prompt('How are you today?');

Reminder:

You can enclose your string with either double quotes or single quotes provided that they match each other. Errors are committed with unmatched quotes.

3. An array of tourist places in the U.S.

var touristPlacesUs;

touristPlacesUs = ['Hollywood', 'Statue of Liberty', 'Grand Canyon', 'Walt Disney World', 'Golden Gate Bridge'];

See image below:

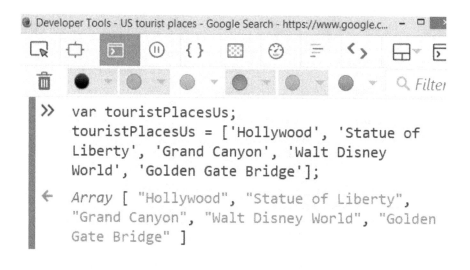

4. A multi-dimensional array of your answer to no. 3.

var touristPlacesUs;

touristPlacesUs = [

['Hollywood', 'actors', 'actresses'],

['Statue of Liberty', 'democracy', 'torch']

['Grand Canyon', 'rock formations', 'trails']

['Walt Disney World', 'Lion King', 'Aladdin']

['Golden Gate Bridge', 'structure', 'landmark']

];

See next image:

```
       Elements  Console  Sources  Network  »        ⋮

   ⊘  ▽  top  ▼  ☐ Preserve log

>  var touristPlacesUs;
   touristPlacesUs = [
       ["Hollywood", "actors", "actresses"],
       ["Statue of Liberty", "democracy", "torch"],
       ["Grand Canyon", "rock formations", "trails"],
       ["Walt Disney World", "Lion King", "Aladdin"],
       ["Golden Gate Bridge", "structure", "landmark"]
   ];
<  ▶ [Array[3], Array[3], Array[3], Array[3], Array[3]]
>  |
```

5. Obtaining and displaying the value of index 3 in your answer to no. 3.

   Document.write(touristPlacesUs[3]);

See image below:

6. Changing the index 2 of your answer to no. 3 to "Yellowstone National Park".

> *touristPlacesUs[2] = 'Yellowstone National Park';*

See image below:

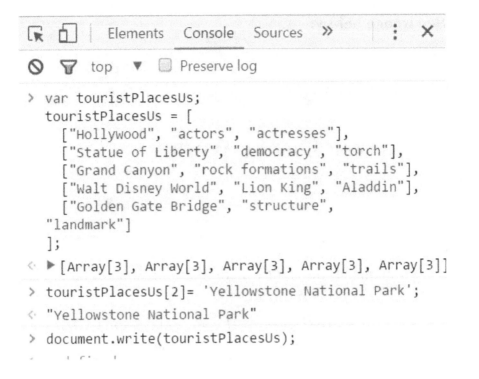

```
>  var touristPlacesUs;
   touristPlacesUs = [
      ["Hollywood", "actors", "actresses"],
      ["Statue of Liberty", "democracy", "torch"],
      ["Grand Canyon", "rock formations", "trails"],
      ["Walt Disney World", "Lion King", "Aladdin"],
      ["Golden Gate Bridge", "structure",
   "landmark"]
   ];
<  ▶ [Array[3], Array[3], Array[3], Array[3], Array[3]]
>  touristPlacesUs[2]= 'Yellowstone National Park';
<  "Yellowstone National Park"
>  document.write(touristPlacesUs);
```

You can display the changes to check if the data was indeed change to Yellowstone National Park by using the code:

Document.write(touristPlacesUs);

When you execute or press 'Enter', the values of the array will appear on the page. See image below:

Hollywood,actors,actresses,Statue of Liberty,democracy,torch,Yellowstone National Park,Walt Disney World,Lion King,Aladdin,Golden Gate Bridge,structure,landmark

Indeed, 'Yellowstone National Park' is now included in the list.

7. Displaying the date and time during the moment you're answering this quiz.

   var today = new Date();

   document.write(today);

This will display the date and time on your web page.

8. A variable named 'employees', and define the variable.

   var employees;

   employees   =   ["Callaghan",   "Denton", "Statham"];

See image below:

```
Elements   Console   Sources   »

top                              ▼   Preserve l

> var employees;
  employees = ["Callaghan", "Denton", "Statham"];
< ► ["Callaghan", "Denton", "Statham"]
> |
```

9. Solving the 10^{15} expression using the JavaScript 'Console'.

$$10**15$$

See image below:

10. Printing or displaying the result of your answer to no. 8.

document.write(employees);

See image below:

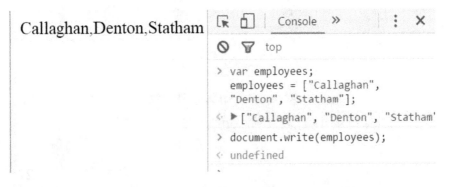

Matching Type

Match column B with column A

Column A
Column B

1. _G_ Containers for data program/code   A.

2. _K_True or false data   B. (=)

3. _J_ Symbols that enclose strings brackets   C.

4. _C_ Symbols that enclose arrays comma   D.

5. _I_ Symbol for equal value   E. var

6. _B_ Symbol to assign values statements   F.

7. _H_ Indicates that the statement is variables   G.

    done
    semicolon   H.

8. _D_ Separates values from one another   I. (==)

9. _E_ The keyword for variable quotes   J.

10. _A_ A group of JavaScript statements Boolean   K.

    L. VAR

M.
strings

N. <=>

Conclusion

You have now the basic knowledge about JavaScript that would help you proceed to more advance lessons.

Also, you will be able to create simple JavaScript codes on your own. Try working with your Google Chrome and Mozilla 'Console' and experiment with your codes to find out what you can do.

Obviously, this book has some difficult topics for advance learners that were not discussed, such as 'form validation of emails, text fields and other data of web page users', and other in-depth topics about JavaScript. But certainly, you have learned the basics.

Eventually, you have to accept the great challenge of creating your own web page and using all the codes you have learned from this book.

Start coding now and have fun!